MAP OF GARDENS AND FOUNTAINS

A   Visitors' entrance. Carriage Courtyard
B   Entrance to the Royal Collegiate Church.
    Plaza de Palacio
C   Entrance to Gardens. Horseshoe Courtyard
D   Fountain Courtyard
🛍🏛 Book and Gift Shop

AREA AROUND THE PALACE

E   Medio Punto Gardens
F   Old *Casa de Damas*. Tapestry Museum
G   Old *Casa de las Cocinas*
H   Old *Casa de Músicos*
I   Old *Casa de Canónigos*
J   Arco del Infante arch
K   Casa de Oficios
L   1844 building

GARDENS

AXIS OF THE WINDS

1   Lower Grove of the Winds
2   Fountain of Aeolus Dominating the Winds
3   Upper Grove of the Winds

AXIS OF THE PARTERRE AND NEW CASCADE

4   Palace Terrace and Parterre
5   New Cascade. Fountain of Amphitrite
6   Fountain of the Three Graces
7   Marble Summer House

AXIS OF THE HORSE-RACE

8   The *Ría* or Old Cascade
9   Grove of the Shells (9 and 10)
    Fountain of the Shells
10 Fountain of the Fan
11 Fountain of Neptune
12 Pond of the Rivers Ebro and Segre
13 Fountain of Apollo and Minerva
14 The Half Moon
15 Boulingrins of Andromeda
16 Fountain of Andromeda
17 Parterre of Andromeda

AXIS OF LA SELVA

18 Fountain of La Selva
19 Groves of La Selva
20 Calle de la Botica Gate
21 Nocturnal Grove
    (advance booking required)
22 El Potosí Gate
23 El Potosí Garden
24 Casa de las Flores Gate
25 Casa de las Flores Garden and Pavilion

OTHER AREAS REQUIRING ADVANCE BOOKING

26 Octagonal Grove
27 The Maze
28 The Apiary
29 Kitchen Gardens and Plant Nurseries

EL MAR AND THE WOOD

30 Calle Honda

OCHO CALLES SECTOR

31 Oval Steps
32 Square Pond
33 Canastillo Fountain
34 La Canal Grove
35 Fountain of La Taza (Upper, Tritons)
36 Fountain of La Taza (Lower, Nereids)
37 Plaza de las Ocho Calles
38 Plaza of Apollo and the Muses
39 Plaza of the Muses
40 Fountains of the Dragons (Upper and Lower)
41 Fountain of Latona
42 Fountain of the Baths of Diana
43 Valsaín Gate

AXIS OF FAMA

44 Parterre of Fame
45 Fountain of Fame
46 Grove of Fame

OTHER KITCHEN AND VEGETABLE GARDENS

47 Grove of Melancholy
48 Partida de la Reina
    (Royal Pharmacy Garden)

Real Sitio de La Granja de San Ildefonso and Riofrío

JOSÉ LUIS SANCHO

JUAN RAMÓN APARICIO

REALES SITIOS DE ESPAÑA

© PATRIMONIO NACIONAL, 2014
Palacio Real de Madrid
Bailén, s/n
28071 Madrid
Tel. 91 547 53 50

© Texts: José Luis Sancho Gaspar (pp. 9-50 and 84-94)
Juan Ramón Aparicio (pp. 50-84)

© Photographs: Patrimonio Nacional / Félix Lorrio
Palacios y Museos / José Barea

N.I.P.O.: 006-14-024-9
I.S.B.N.: 978-84-7120-402-8 (1st ed., 5th impr.)
Legal Deposit: M-8945-2014

Coordination and production: PALACIOS Y MUSEOS
Design and layout: Myriam López Consalvi
Translation: Mervyn Samuel / Laura Suffield /
Nigel Williams
Photograph setting: Lucam
Printed by: Artes Gráficas Palermo

Front cover illustration: View of the Royal Palace of
La Granja from the Fountain of the Three Graces.

Back cover illustration: Decorative motif with a Chinese
dragon. The Lacquer Room. Royal Palace of La Granja.

Impreso en España, *Printed in Spain*

Contents

Presentation

PATRIMONIO NACIONAL is the institution which manages those properties of the State which are at the service of the Crown for performing representative functions as commended by the Constitution and Laws of Spain.

The institution manages a number of Palaces, as well as several Monasteries and Convents founded by Spanish monarchs, all of great historical, artistic and cultural importance and, most significantly, of great *symbolic value*. The Royal Palaces of Madrid, El Pardo, Aranjuez, San Ildefonso and La Almudaina are used as residential and representative buildings as was intended when they were built centuries ago and it is here where His Majesty the King performs his duties as Head of State, particularly in the Royal Palace of Madrid, where this *symbolic value* is felt most strongly, as the official residence of the Crown.

In harmony with these functions, the other buildings and properties which make up *Patrimonio Nacional* have a decidedly cultural purpose and are places of study and research, as well as being open to the general public.

Both the buildings and the Spanish royal collections (27 in all, ranging from fans to tools and which include silverware, paintings, tapestries, furniture, musical instruments, clocks, etc.) are remarkable for a number of characteristics which go to make *Patrimonio Nacional* a unique cultural institution: their *particular purpose*, as they are still considered valid for representative use by the Crown; their *historical authenticity*, as they are all pieces which have been ordered, acquired or offered as gifts at some time for that particular place; their *originality*, which can be seen by the absence of replicas and imitations, and their *extraordinary artistic, historical and symbolic value*.

The combination of such impressive characteristics makes it clear to the visitor that *Patrimonio Nacional* is much more than a simple museum.

The Spanish Royal Palaces are surrounded by approximately 20,500 hectares of open land. Around 500 hectares are given over to gardens or farmland, while the remaining 20,000 hectares are forest, divided between El Pardo, La Herrería and Riofrío and part of which is open to the general public. These woodlands, mainly of the biotype *Mediterranean forest*, are of renowned ecological importance, the value of which is at a par with the monuments found in their midst.

The Royal Monasteries and Convents have been attended by the same religious orders since their foundation, with the exception of San Lorenzo de El Escorial, originally of the Hieronymite Order, which was passed over to the Augustinian Order following the sale of Church lands in the 19th century. They enjoy particular importance in the history of Spain, as their origin dates back to the particular patronage of the monarchs of the era.

By being open to the general public, not only do these buildings fulfil a cultural purpose, they allow the Spanish people to capture their symbolic value, identify with it and consider themselves a legatee of the vast historical and artistic treasures which make up the properties of *Patrimonio Nacional*.

Collected over the centuries by the Crown, their influence in the cultural identity of Spain has been, and still is, decisive.

Introduction

By the Middle Ages, the kings of Castile, who often resided in the city of Segovia, were hunting in the woodlands situated at the foot of the Guadarrama Mountains, and particularly in the Valsaín district, where Henry IV built the palace known as the *Casa del Bosque* ("House in the Wood"); in 1450 he constructed another more modest refuge, and next to it a chapel dedicated to St Ildephonsus. In 1477, Ferdinand and Isabella the Catholic granted this shrine and the adjacent property to the Hieronymite monks of the Monastery of El Parral, in Segovia, who converted it into an estate for recreation (p. 40).

Successive kings continued to hunt regularly at Valsaín and around 1717 Philip V, while hunting around the estate of the Hieronymites "fell in love" with the place: he had found the ideal spot to retire from the world, for his of mind, worn down by neurasthenia, longed for tranquillity.

The first Spanish Bourbon

Philip of Bourbon, Duke of Anjou, was the great-grandson of Philip IV, whose eldest daughter, María Teresa, had married Louis XIV; this explains why in 1700, when the Spanish branch of the Habsburgs came to an end, Charles II declared the Duke of Anjou his universal heir in his will. However, his ascent to the throne of Spain proved no simple matter, as treaties signed previously between the great power and the opposing interests of England, the Netherlands and the Austrian Empire on the one hand, and France and Spain on the other, resulted in the War of the Spanish Succession that lasted until the Peace of Utrecht in 1713.

The Duke of Anjou, born in 1683, had been brought up at the splendid court of his grandfather, Louis XIV, and as he was the second son of *Monseigneur Le Gran Dauphin*, the heir to the throne (who died in 1711), and it was not considered likely that in his lifetime he would ever succeed to the throne, care was taken in his upbringing to rid him of any thoughts of aspiring to it. Who then would have supposed that his brothers were to die in 1713? And that, therefore, if his only nephew Louis XV were to have died as a child, which almost happened, he would have occupied the throne of France? His phlegmatic temperament facilitated his education, and he proved to be a pious, tranquil, kind and somewhat introverted prince; intelligent, and very fond of physical exercise and hunting, like all his family.

When at the age of seventeen the Duke of Anjou became Philip V, King of Spain and the Indies, he began to suffer a process of psychological decline made more acute by the prolonged war. Fortunately, his insecure nature led him to seek refuge in his wives, both of whom had strong personalities: María Luisa of Savoy, who died in 1714, and Isabella Farnese, whom he married in the same year. The latter's desire to endow her numerous sons with kingdoms and possessions in Italy was not sufficient to persuade this man, whose spirits had already sunk by the age of little more than thirty, away from the idea of relinquishing power.

The Royal Seat, retreat of Philip V

For relaxation, the King went hunting ever more frequently in the royal woodlands of El Pardo and Valsaín, accompanied by the Queen and his faithful *Master of the Horse*, the Duque del Arco. In 1718, impressed by the abundance of game and the beauty of the landscape, he decided to buy La Granja de San Ildefonso from the Hieronymites and convert it into a *Royal Seat* for his retirement. As was

The axis of Fame with the Parterre, Fountain and Grove, from the clock tower in the Horseshoe Courtyard.

appropriate to a princely mansion in the countryside, the most impressive feature would be the gardens, to the extent of permitting comparison with those he had left behind in France.

The purchase of La Granja was completed in 1720, and in 1723 and 1735 further land was acquired from the Noble Committee of Lineages and City of Segovia, but this does not seem to have determined the overall plan of the new estate. The definitive extension on the basis of the original nucleus was made in accordance with the King's wishes and the plans drawn up by his architects. Only in this way is it possible to explain the regularity of the overall perimeter: a rectangle enclosed within strong walls of rough stone.

More than two thirds of the space within this rectangle is devoted to the gardens; the Royal Palace and the Collegiate Church separate these from the lower third, where the buildings used as accommodation for the *royal entourage* were constructed. The overall unity achieved arises from the coherent design of the garden, the spatial axes being arranged within an enclosed area.

The construction of Palace and garden, in the initial form designed for the King's retirement, was undertaken between 1720 and the end of 1723; on the 15th of August in the latter year it was announced that "The King has resolved to return to this Seat from El Escorial on the 9th of September next, and to come to live with the Queen in this Grange... the Palace and accommodation for the household staff of the Family are completed, cleared and clean". On the 10th of January 1724, Philip V declared at San Ildefonso that he had abdicated in favour of his son, Louis I: however, Louis's premature death in the August of that same year meant that the "King Father" was obliged to return to the throne.

La Granja had to be adapted to this change, as from being the residence of an ex-sovereign it had become the favourite *Royal Seat* of the reigning Monarch. The palace, which was initially a small building, had to be enlarged, as was the garden at the expense of the park, with the addition of new and magnificent fountains. The following years saw ceaseless construction

and decoration, halted only in 1746 by the death of the King who, since returning from his journey around Andalusia (the period known as the "royal lustrum" of 1729-1734) had spent every summer in the artificial paradise he had created, where, if tranquillity eluded him, it was certainly not because his senses were not satisfied. His hearing was caressed by the harmony of Farinelli's songs and the play of water in the garden; his sight by the spectacle of the waters animated by the sculptures of Frémin and Thierry, the architecture of Juvarra, the collection of antique statues that had once belonged to Queen Christina of Sweden, and the superb collection of paintings, the best of which are now in the Prado Museum; his taste

Louis-Michel van Loo: The Family of Philip V. *Copy by Lozano Valle. 19th century. Portrait Gallery.* ▲

and smell by the products of the orchards and kitchen gardens.

The Summer "Sojourn" at San Ildefonso

WHEN PHILIP V died, his widow Isabella Farnese was granted lifelong use of La Granja, where she lived throughout the reign of her stepson Ferdinand VI (1746-1759). During this period she felt no need for the new Royal Palace built on her personal domain of Riofrío. The accession of her son Charles III to the throne signified the return of all its glory to the *Royal Seat*, for once again, during the next two centuries, it was to be the residence of the Monarch and the setting for the splendours of the court in the warmest months of the year, between the Spring "Sojourn" at Aranjuez and the Autumn one at El Escorial.

During the reigns of Charles III (with the laying out of the town and the construction of large buildings for the entourage) and Ferdinand VII, the Sojourn at La Granja was especially brilliant, but during the reign of Isabella II the railway and the fashion for sea bathing began to attract the Royal Family towards the beaches of the North: firstly to San Sebastián (where the Queen Regent Maria Cristina of Austria built the Palace of Miramar) and then to Santander. The Palace of La Magdalena, a gift from the city of Santander to Alfonso XIII in 1912, became the favourite place for the summer, particularly after the terrible fire that destroyed a large part of the San Ildefonso Palace in 1918. Nevertheless, court life was still resplendent at La Granja during the reign of Alfonso XIII: here several of his children were born, including *Don* Juan, father of King Juan Carlos I, and the King's aunt, the Infanta Isabel (known as *la Chata* – "Snub-nose"), maintained her fondness for the Royal Seat.

The entrance to the Royal Seat: the Plaza de Palacio

THE PUERTA de Segovia (Segovia Gate), with its three sections of wrought-iron railings and gilded decoration designed by José Díaz Gamones in 1767, constitutes the main entrance to San Ildefonso. From it, a straight avenue leads to the Plaza de Palacio which is surrounded by some of the 18th-century buildings intended to house the *royal entourage*.

As Philip V did not order work on the urban layout of San Ildefonso to be implemented until 1766, it was completed in the reign of Charles III in 1788 by the architect José Díaz Gamones. The most important buildings are those erected as quarters for the servants and the king's ministers and other dignitaries. These buildings included:

The Old *Casa de Oficios,* later known as the *Casa de Damas,* which contained the monarchs' private rooms from the time of Charles IV until the fire of 1918; it was partially rebuilt and converted into the **Tapestry Museum.** The *Casa de Oficios,* built by Procaccini (1725) and rebuilt by Sacchetti after a fire in 1740 and restored in 1941. The *Casa de Canónigos,* which was affected by fires in 1754, 1787, 1808 and 1918; the current building dates from the reign of Ferdinand VII, although it was converted into dwellings in 1963. The *Caballerizas Reales,* which date from 1738 and were restored in 1945 and 1985. Opposite is the *Cuartel de Guardias de Corps,* which was designed by Juan Esteban in 1764 and now stands in ruins. The *Casa de Infantes,* dating from 1770 and built by Gamones for the servants of the Infantes *Don* Gabriel and *Don* Antonio, sons of Charles III; this is the Royal Seat's largest, most monumental building and is now undergoing reconstruction with a view to conversion into a *Parador* (state hotel). The

Real Fábrica de Cristales, built in 1770 and restored in 1982.

Built by Gamones in 1774, the *Casa de Gentileshombres* is now privately owned, having been sold in 1870, as were many other buildings belonging to the king such as Scotti's Administration building, the Estanco building – all in the Plaza de Palacio – as well as the *Alhajas* ("Treasury"), *Almacenes* ("Warehouse), *Cocinas* ("Kitchens"), *Cocheras* ("Coach House") and public buildings – like the *Hospital Viejo* ("Old Hospital"), which is now the Town Hall – originally built for the Crown, and the barracks.

Further up, a large space opens out, dominated by the west façade of the Royal Palace, from the centre of which the apse and towers of the **Royal Collegiate Church** project.

The Plaza had no trees until 1853, when the avenues of horse chestnuts were planted, adjoining the lower edge of the **Medio Punto Gardens,** created in the years following the pseudo-landscape style of the squares of Paris. In 1877 the *head gardener* Antonio Testard supervised the planting of conifers, then considered ornamental exotics, which have grown superbly. They include several very notable Spanish firs *(Abies pinsapo),* and above all the two enormous sequoias *(Sequoiadendron gigantum)* which, like natural obelisks, keep the Palace spires company.

To the right of the Royal Collegiate Church is the *Arco del Infante,* an arch so named due to the fact that the apartments of *Don* Felipe, subsequently Duke of Parma, were situated above it. This area was later occupied by Philip's

Aerial view of the Royal Seat of La Granja de San Ildefonso with the Puerta de Segovia entrance to the Royal Palace and gardens. ▲

brother Louis and later still by the Infante *Don Gabriel*. The arch joins the Palace to the **Casa de Oficios,** where the king's senior ministers were accommodated. Opposite the main gate and the Calle del Rey are the three beautiful wrought-iron gates that form the entrance to the garden; they were made by Sebastián de Flores (1723) and Fernando Garrido.

The Gardens

"IF ONE goes to live in the country it is to be able to have a larger and more magnificent garden. In this case the best thing is to be content with a small house, accompanied by a large garden," said Dézallier, the French garden theorist. Following this principle, at La Granja the garden was more important than the Palace. Philip V followed the policy of specialization in work rather than unity of taste, and instead of ordering the design of both house and garden from a single artist, he commissioned his French architect René Carlier to lay out the garden, and his Spanish *Master of Works*, Teodoro Ardemans, to build the Palace.

From the time of Philip's return to the throne in 1724, this difference between garden and house, between European and Spanish forms, became less obvious due to the process of extension of the residence which acquired exterior façades in the Italian manner, while the garden increased in size and new ornamentation was added to it. The relationship between the two changed in the direction of greater balance, but in any case the protagonist

▲ *Aerial view of the Royal Palace of La Granja featuring the Medio Punto Gardens and the Plaza de Palacio.*

continued to be the garden, which is still maintained intact with all its sculptures. It is from the garden that the finest views of the façades can be seen.

Before starting our walk, it is well worth focusing on some of the background history of the palace and garden.

La Granja in the history of French and Spanish gardening

THE FORMAL garden in the French manner, whose popularity spread throughout Europe in the late 17th and the 18th century, had reached its zenith during the reign of Louis XIV, due to the creations of Le Nôtre, among which Versailles is the outstanding example. However, as an immediate precedent to La

Granja one could point to another garden of the Sun King, less well known as it was destroyed during the Revolution: Marly, where the King spent periods of rest.

At La Granja, Philip V did not aim to emulate the vast and regal stage set created by his grandfather at Versailles, but rather to construct a palace with gardens for his retirement. It is not surprising that for this purpose he had Marly in mind, in view of the similarity of its aim, the physical features of its site, and the fact that as an artistic creation it had been built more recently than Versailles and it was where the principal sculptors summoned to La Granja had previously worked.

On the basis of this model, he wanted a garden in the French manner, the magnificence of which must be worthy of a Spanish monarch

Sebastián de Flores and Fernando Garrido: gilded forged iron gates (c. 1723-30). ▲
Entrance to the Palace garden via the Horseshoe Courtyard terrace.

capable of such a "heroic" abdication; a garden rich in sculptures and fountains, laid out in accordance with the latest style, differing from that of Versailles in that it brought new interpretative nuances to Le Nôtre's concepts.

The decisive factors for the form of the garden were the terrain, the position of the Palace, and the existence of three areas with well-differentiated functions and characteristics: the areas for kitchen produce, fruit and flowers (potagers), the formal garden (jardin de propreté) and the park (parc). The area chosen, the site of the Palace and therefore of the garden, and almost certainly the exact limits of the property, were decided personally and, indeed, it could be said capriciously, by Philip V. It was the Monarch who made the choice, and not his technical experts who had to turn difficulties into advantages: a stony site rising upwards from the Palace, but falling away on the left towards the course of a stream.

The layout of the garden, the unusual features of which are explained by these conditioning factors and by the taste of the period, is due to the French architect René Carlier who before his premature death in August 1722 had time to leave it designed in its entirety and to a large extent completed. On the rising land in front of the Palace, Carlier planned a formal garden laid out in several adjoining parallel axes, dominated by four principal ones: the **Grove of the Winds, the Main Cascade, the Horse-race** and the *Ría,* which is a canalized stream that crosses the northern transversal axis of **La Selva.** Beside the garden is a park with eight avenues converging at a central circus where hunters could meet, lacking the ornamental character of the garden and separated from it by a wall; and in the lateral areas several *potagers* or reserved areas for cultivating vegetables, fruit or flowers. The division into garden and park,

separated by the Calle de la Medianería (and originally also by a wall running all along this avenue) was emphasised by various differences: the park area, or **Ocho Calles,** was planted with elms and had lateral promenades, while to the north of the Medianería there were no elms, the avenues were narrower and they were planted with linden trees. All this greenery was separated from the Palace by the Calle de Valsaín, which extended along the Palace terrace and formed the basic transversal axis of the garden, around which the groves and low *potagers* were arranged. Following the death of Louis I and Philip V's return to the throne, the park was incorporated into the garden and this addition together with that of other groves adjoining the Ocho Calles was embellished with even more magnificent new fountains and sculptures when the southern axis of **Fame** was created.

The fountains and ornamental sculpture

THE *JEUX d'eau* of the fountains and the sculptures that bring them to life are the great protagonists of San Ildefonso's gardens.

The abundance of water was one of the greatest attractions of the place for Philip V, as it allowed him to fill the gardens with the kind of spectacular fountains which had become increasingly popular from the Italian Renaissance (Tivoli, Boboli) to Louis XIV, whose engineers took hydraulic artifice to extremes of refinement limited only by scarcity of water or problems with pumping, as occurred at Versailles.

At La Granja, water of great purity, crystalline and very abundant, flowing from the mountain, was like a rough diamond awaiting the French experts who cut it to the King's taste. The construction of the general reservoir (*El Mar*), a further six smaller ones,

The Horse-Race axis with the Fountain of Neptune pond, from the Palace's main floor.
Pages 16-17, the façade of the Royal Palace facing the Parterre, viewed from the top of the New Cascade axis. ▶

and a distribution system of various kilometres of iron pipes, are the main features of the hydraulic system that is still intact today. By simple pressure and without the assistance of pumps, it raises the jets of water to heights of over forty metres.

The sculptures constitute the most extensive and best-preserved collection of this type of French decorative work from the last years of Louis XIV and the Regency, given that Marly no longer exists in its original state. Made in a relatively short space of time, and therefore very homogeneous, they are mainly the work of two artists: René Frémin and Jean Thierry, who were summoned in 1721 and directed a large team of assistants including nine workmen, six marble cutters, two mould makers and a chaser, among others.

René Frémin (Paris 1672-1744), a pupil of Girardon, studied in Rome, was a Professor at the Paris Academy and created numerous works for Versailles and Marly; some are now in the Louvre. Appointed "first sculptor" in 1727, he continued at La Granja until 1738. His works have considerable strength and character.

Jean Thierry (Lyon 1669-1739), was a less outstanding personality than Frémin, with whom he collaborated at Versailles and made many now vanished works for Marly. He returned to France in 1728. Though without his colleague's vigour, his work is delicate (at times, somewhat precious) and harmonious in composition, with the gestures and movements of his figures restrained in character.

When Frémin returned to France, he was replaced as head of sculpture by Jacques Bousseau, who died soon after in 1740, but in a short period managed to oversee the execution of various marble sculptures following his own designs or those of Frémin. In addition to other projects, he also completed the huge task of making all the models for the sculptures for the **Fountain of the Baths of Diana.** This work was completed after his death by the craftsmen in the sculpture workshop, notable among whom were Pierre Puthois and Hubert Dumandré, the latter the leading figure in a family of sculptors who worked for the royal house until well into the 19th century.

The process of realising the sculptures was a complex one involving many stages, from the "invention" of the model to its final realisation, but enough information has survived to enable us to attribute them securely to the different hands involved: their respective makers are indicated here with the initial of their surname in brackets.

The high quality of the pieces is characteristic of the decorative sense and formal elegance of the Rococo, though Frémin and Thierry often sought inspiration in designs by Charles Le Brun which fell within the heroic style of the century of Louis XIV.

The workshops were installed at Valsaín. For essentially economic reasons, the sculptures were finally not cast in bronze; instead, use was made of lead with a reddish varnish imitating bronze (and gilded in a few small details), as was then a common practice in France, from where the paint was ordered. It was then applied by the specialist Jean La Coste. Since the beginning of this century an extensive campaign has been under way in the garden to restore plants, fountains and statues; in the case of the latter, with the recovery of the original *bronze varnish* finish.

When do the fountains work?

THE CUSTOM at La Granja is that all the fountains play only on the 25th of August, feast of St Louis (patron of the Royal Seat), but some also work in the springtime and summer.

R. Frémin, J. Bousseau, P, Puthois and H. Dumandré: the Fountain of the Baths of Diana, 1737-45. ▶
Detail of the jeux d'eau. Ocho Calles sector.

Recently, they usually play on Wednesdays, Saturdays and Sundays, alternating each week between one or other of the two following groups described on the pages indicated in brackets:

- **The Horse-Race** (28), **the Main Cascade** (26), **the Winds** (24 and 34) and **Fame** (40).
- **The Canastillo** (36), **Latona** (38), **the Baths of Diana** (39) and **Fame** (40).

Since a water-recycling system was installed in the Baths of Diana in 1990, this fountain plays for one hour on summer evenings at weekends, and the floodlit garden is most agreeable at such times. The visitor is particularly recommended to see the **Horse-Race,** the **Canastillo** and the **Latona:** in order to do so it is important to allow enough time once inside the gardens and not to get lost between the last two.

A walk around the garden

THE SOUTH façade of the Palace opens to form the "courtyard of honour" or **Horseshoe Courtyard,** leading to the long Parterre of Fame, at the far end of which is the great fountain from which its name is taken. With its urns, sculptures and marble benches, it offers a fine view from the gilded wrought-iron balustrade (p. 42).

Although the wrought-iron gateway through which we entered dates from the reign of Philip V, it was not installed here until 1844, when this area achieved its present appearance with the building of the steps and long bench with a wrought-iron back separating it from the parterre, as the two levels were previously linked by a staircase and grass ramps.

To the right is the Calle de Valsaín, until 1724 the main entrance for the monarchs

The axis of Fame from the clock tower, with the Horseshoe Courtyard and Terrace facing the Parterre, ▲
the Fountain and the Grove of Fame.

arriving from the old Valsaín Palace, separating the Parterre of Fame from the great design of the Ocho Calles ("Eight Avenues") which is the start of the park, while in front of us it ascends to *El Mar* ("the Sea"), the Wood ("El Bosque") and the Calle de la Medianería. From this point all directions are inviting for a walk, but the one most in accordance with the original sense of the garden and with the process of its creation is the one suggested here.

Other possibilities are to walk up the Medianería as far as *El Mar* and the park, (p. 35) leaving the Ocho Calles (p. 36) or to go to the Baths of Diana (p. 39) by way of either the Calle de Valsaín or the Parterre of Fame.

As the Calle de Valsaín passes in front of the main façade of the Palace towards the gardens, it becomes a paved terrace, decorated

with sculptural groups of *amorinos* and *sphinxes* in painted lead (F). The first linden grove or plantation, known as the **Bosquete de los Vientos** ("Grove of the Winds") because of the fountain in its upper part (and which we shall look at later), is very close to the building, a situation praised by the garden theoreticians of the time: "Groves are especially pleasant when close to the house, as in this way one finds shade immediately on going out, as well as the freshness they give to the rooms, a highly desirable thing in the hot season" (Dézallier). Next we reach the **Palace Parterre,** which is as wide as the original width of the Palace itself when first constructed (corresponding to the central section of the present residence's façade). Its axis is prolonged in the monumental **New Cascade,** surmounted by the

▲　*René Frémin: the Fountain of Aeolus dominating the Winds, on the Grove of the Winds axis in front of the southeast wing of the Palace.*

René Frémin: a painted lead Sphinx or Chimaera on the Parterre Terrace. ▶

Fountain of the Three Graces and the Pavilion or **Marble Summer House.** Here the relationship with Marly is particularly evident.

The Parterre is decorated with lead urns and flanked by marble benches and statues: on the right are Autumn or Bacchus, America, Summer or Ceres (T); to the left are Africa, Milon of Croton and Fidelity (F). **The Cascade,** whose sculptures include the **Rivers Tagus and Guadiana** appearing astonished at such royal magnificence (T), were finished and functioned for the first time in 1723: they underwent major restoration work in the second half of the 19th century. In the lower basin, the **Fountain of Amphitrite** group (T) is an allusion to Queen Isabella Farnese as the companion of Neptune, a personification of Philip V in the full dominion of his kingdom (p. 32). The Cascade is surmounted by two groups of animals and another two of amorinos on sea horses plus three fantastic mascarons spouting water (F).

Although it is probably better to turn back towards the Palace at this point, the visitor can also carry on up to the pavilion (p. 32), admiring the statues flanking the Cascade and arranged in pairs, one to the left and the other to the right: the Glory of Princes (T), and Magnificence (F); Asia (F) and Europe (T); Winter (T) and a Shepherd (F); Spring (T) and Diana (F). The twenty-eight lead urns, painted to imitate white marble, which alternate with the sculptures in this parterre and also on the ascent to the Fountain of the Three Graces and in the Fountain of Andromeda, replaced those made by Thierry in white marble, which were moved to Aranjuez in 1797 on the order of Charles IV.

▲ Vertumnus removing his mask before Pomona, *the central group of statues in the Fountain of La Selva in front of the northeast wing of the Palace. Axis of La Selva.*

The King ordered Luigi Poggetti to make these replacements, which were installed in 1804.

Four of Thierry's urns are now on the main staircase in the Royal Palace in Madrid, while the remainder are still at Aranjuez: this splendid group is the only missing part of the decorative sculpture scheme in the gardens as it was completed during the reign of Philip V.

On both sides of the parterre, and contrasting with its character as an open space, the linden groves form closed masses which complement it and form small chambers or rooms of vegetation; all of this part was already planted by June 1722.

Continuing along the Palace Terrace, on the right is the magnificent perspective of the Horse-Race (which we will return to later), and at the end from the top of a flight of steps we can see how the transverse axis of the garden is prolonged downwards to the **Fountain of La Selva,** the **Groves of La Selva,** the bridge over the *Ría,* the **Nocturnal Groves** (*L'Anneau Tournant*), the **Potosí Garden** (*Le Potager*), the **Garden and Pavilion of the *Casa de las Flores*** and beyond them the vegetable garden and Maze. It is probably better to walk down to these features later, but the visitor who would like to do so now and then return to the present route should turn to page 35.

The **Fountain of La Selva** has many high jets arranged closely together producing the effect of a sheaf or gavel (*gerbe* in French), and a corrupt version of this word gave rise to its Spanish name. Both the sheaf-like form of the jets of water and the mythological figures of Vertumnus and *Pomona* occupying its centre

Jean Thierry: Naiad and zephyrs holding a fish. *Fountain of the Fan. Grove of the Shells. Axis of the Horse-Race.* ▲

allude to the royal kitchen gardens and orchards situated beyond the *Ría*, with magnificent railings by Sebastián de Flores, dating from the time when this area was laid out. Also very fine is the railing stretching from this point to the Calle de la Botica. The bridge is a harmonious creation of Carlier, built by the stonemason Andrés Collado. The marble figures or "terms" standing out against the hornbeam hedge are by four of the principal French sculptors who remained at La Granja after the departure of Frémin and Thierry and the death of Bousseau.

From this same balcony of La Selva, two of the great longitudinal axes of the garden may be appreciated, parallel to the Calle de la Medianería and to the axis of the Parterre Cascade, whose pathway leads uphill: the **Ría** or **Old Cascade,** and the **Horse-Race.** These views, whose perspectival recession was blocked by the mountains, went against the canons of Baroque taste which generally favoured open, unlimited views. Philip V's unusually picturesque aesthetic led him to desire the gardens to be oriented towards the mountains, a choice which can partly be explained by a wish to take advantage of the most important feature of the site: the abundance of running water from the mountains which could be stored in the larger upper reservoir known as **El Mar,** and which could then be used to create the great cascades which ran down towards the palace.

The **Ría,** with a series of stepped waterfalls in the manner of cascades, is the course of a natural stream canalized by Carlier when the garden was created; above this watercourse he contained the natural slope of the land by means of a strong stone wall supporting a long terrace, the whole length of which is delimited by a fine wrought-iron railing by Sebastián de Flores, from which the whole of the *Ría* can be viewed.

René Frémin: the Fountain of Neptune pond in front of the Palace. Axis of the Horse-Race. ▲

This long terraced space, arranged on various levels rising from that of the lower floor of the palace, serves as the setting for the most grandiose aquatic spectacle of La Granja, the succession of fountains popularly known as the **Horse-Race,** which includes the **Fountains of the Shells** and **of the Fan,** of **Neptune,** of **Apollo** or the **Lyre,** and the **Dragons** in the **Half Moon** of the *Ría*, forming the base of the *Ría* at the termination of its highest part, and continuing visually on to the **Fountain of Andromeda.**

In the first place, lines of linden trees with high hornbeam "walls" used to form the **Grove of the Shells** with three "rooms" which houses three fountains: the two small circular ones known as the **Shell** fountain once had basins which were decorated with "shells and other sea products or spoils" (T); between them, a square

pond – the **Fountain of the Fan** – contains a *water-nymph* (T) clutching a fish and accompanied by *zephyrs* (from the fish's mouth emerge jets of water in the shape of a fan, giving the fountain its name). However, rather than the picturesque, miniaturised delicacy which the proximity of the Palace imposed on these fountains, the protagonists of this long ascendant perspective silhouetted against the mountain are the figures of the following large fountains.

In the **Fountain of Neptune,** at the centre of a long rectangular pond the god moves imposingly over the waters in a triumphal chariot of shells drawn by sea horses. He is preceded and followed by groups of similar creatures with *tritons*, *cupids*, horns of plenty replete with the fruits of the sea, and *dolphins*, while three vertical and sixteen smaller

René Frémin: The god Neptune in his sea chariot drawn by sea horses. ▲
Detail of the Fountain of Neptune pond. Axis of the Horse-Race.
The Fountain of the Three Graces (R. Frémin), in front of the Marble Summer House (R. Carlier), Axis of the New Cascade. ▶

jets of water emerge from the three groups of figures (F).

The **Rivers Ebro and Segre** (T) flank a *large mascaron* pouring water out into a basin with alternating curved and straight walls situated between the two flights of marble steps ascending to the upper level. This terrace is sloping, so that the large pond in its centre is divided into three cascades. In the first or lower one – the **Fountain of Apollo and Minerva** – are the main sculptures from which its name is derived: *Apollo*, triumphant over the *Serpent Python* lying submissively at his feet, calmly holds his lyre while the *Love of Art*, who seeks his protection, presents him with a laurel wreath, and that of *War* holds a quiver ready to provide him with arrows. *Minerva*, or invincible virtue (whose shield displays the motto, "neither by chance nor by destiny"), who has vanquished *Envy* and *Discord* lying at her feet, holds out an olive branch to Apollo as a symbol of peace (T). On the other cascades are four *groups of small tritons with dragons* (T), and in total there are five high waterspouts.

The mythological themes of this theatrical complex of fountains –including that of Andromeda – take on an unmistakable meaning when considered in their totality. This has to be understood by starting at the most distant scene and passing through the entire "theatre" until coming close to the Palace, where logically more moderate images are more appropriate. The allusions are to the role of Philip V as saviour of the Monarchy and victor over his enemies in the War of the Spanish Succession (Andromeda); as triumphant over rebellion, envy and discord, and protector of the Arts (Apollo); the rivers in the next basin signify the rebellious regions; and finally, absolute lord of his peaceful and extensive dominions (Neptune). This vast succession of allegories recalls the similar use

of these themes in Baroque opera, as in the case of *Naïs* by Rameau (1749), whose aquatic themes make an interesting reference point with regard to La Granja.

Continuing upwards on the railing side, a good view is obtained over the **Ría** or **Old Cascade,** which forms the **Half Moon,** with two huge dragons spouting jets of water around the islet with the basin of Apollo. This curve seems intended so that the visitor, pausing here, has the sensation of living among water. When the Fountain of Andromeda is flowing at the highest point of the *Ría*, together with all the fountains in the perspective towards the Palace, a spectator standing on the islet would have the impression that vegetable matter had turned liquid, in a transformation worthy of Armida's palace.

From the Half Moon, a flight of steps ascends to the top of the axis of the New Cascade: the open space with the **Fountain of the Three Graces,** from which there is a view over the Cascade, the Parterre and the façade of the Palace designed by Juvarra. From the pavilion marking the end of the open space, not only this fine prospect may be enjoyed, but also another in the opposite direction rising up towards *El Mar*, having first descended to the Parterre of Andromeda.

The Pavilion – or **Marble Summer House** as it was called in the 18th century, in allusion to the marble with which its interior is decorated, with pilasters of a composite order – was designed by Carlier but built under the direction of Frémin and Thierry. On its exterior of rose-pink limestone from Sepúlveda, allegories of the *Four Corners of the World* decorate the flat corners, the *Four Seasons* or the *Four Ages of Man* on the mascarons on the bosses, and the *Love of Virtue* at the top, while inside four allegorical female figures (F) allude to its use as a room for enjoying music, which

René Frémin: Perseus saving Andromeda from the sea monster freed by Neptune. ▶
Fountain of Andromeda, on the Axis of the Horse-Race.

was so important at the court of Philip V, who obtained the services of the famous *castrato* Farinelli and encouraged the Italian opera to take root in Spain.

The visitor who now wishes to go on to the Plaza of the Eight Avenues (p. 37), will find to his or her right the **Fountain of Aeolus dominating the Winds** (F), which gives its name to the upper and lower groves and depicts the god with a crown and sceptre and a wineskin enclosing the winds as a symbol of virtue dominating the passions.

The **Parterre of Andromeda** is decorated with lead urns by Frémin, and with four marble sculptures representing *Juno, Neptune, Saturn* and *Ismene* playing the German flute. (F) Crossing the parterre we reach the great **Fountain of Andromeda** (F), which portrays *Perseus* saving the Ethiopian princess from the dragon that had come to devour her when she

was chained to a rock on the instructions of *Juno*. If in this case the hero represents the first Spanish Monarch of the Bourbon dynasty saving the Monarchy, *Minerva*, who is assisting him, refers to France, his principal supporter in the War of Succession. Overcoming the monster with the Medusa head, Perseus has inflicted many wounds from which spring jets of water: hence the name *Pond of the Wounds* given to the small basin slightly further up from which the water flows down to this fountain; the main jet of water reaches a height of 37 metres, but nowadays it is normally inactive.

The Fountain of Andromeda is the highest point of both the *Ría* and the great complex of the Horse-Race, for which the large *treillage* (meaning gallery of wooden latticework) occupying the entire half circumference at the rear of the plaza served as a theatrical backdrop and vantage point. In its place the only features

▲ *René Frémin: the Canastillo Fountain with two of the four phases of the jeux d'eau. Ocho Calles Sector.*

that remain are the marble sculptures of the *Four Elements* and *Pastoral, Lyrical, Heroic and Satirical Poetry*, all by Frémin, except for the first two on the right, which are by Thierry.

Beyond the *treillage*, and contrasting and complementing the preceding parterres, were the **Groves of Andromeda,** which must surely have been intended to contain *cabinets et salons de verdure*; however, this idea was abandoned in 1737, and the order was given to place the four sculptures or "terms" intended for this spot in the groves of La Selva (which we have already seen).

At this point, several different paths can be taken. One possibility is to continue walking around the original garden, returning to the Palace by way of La Selva; in this way one sees the curious **Maze,** designed by Carlier following a plan published by Dézallier. Visitors should try to take care not to get lost in the maze on a very hot day or in bad weather (see the main map). Another possibility, for visitors who would like a long walk beyond the formal garden, is to go up as far as **El Mar,** the name given at La Granja and also at Aranjuez to the pond used to store the water for the fountains. The pine-covered slopes of the Peñalara mountain are reflected in its clear surface and captured the picturesque imagination of the European travellers of the Enlightenment and Romantic periods who visited the gardens. On the bank is the **Gondola House** which was built in 1725 to house the elaborate *ceremonial vessel* which originally belonged to Charles II (now in the Royal Barge Museum at Aranjuez) and which Louis I sent from the Retiro in Madrid in order that Philip V could enjoy boating at La Granja.

The wood surrounding *El Mar* was added in 1735 to the original boundary of the *Royal Seat*, and now offers the visitor a very agreeable one-hour walk.

Either by arriving from the Fountain of Andromeda or descending from *El Mar*, we now find ourselves in the first part of the park, known as the areas of the Eight Avenues, where the avenues were originally planted with oak trees and were of a different width to those in the original *garden* where lime trees predominated, as we have already noted.

The **Oval Steps** of lawn rise from the Parterre of Andromeda to the Calle de la Medianería, which is crossed to reach the **Square Pond;** this was originally intended to supply the New Cascade while *El Mar* (the general water reservoir) was being constructed, and its angled position prevented a regular layout being given to the woodland groves above this line, when in 1728 they were added by Marchand to Carlier's design; the serenity of these waters and the reflection of the massed trees give it a special charm.

Jean Thierry: the Upper Fountain of La Taza (Tritons). Ocho Calles Sector. ▲

The **Canastillo** ("Little Basket") **Fountain** (F) is the simplest one in terms of sculpture, but the play of its waters is the most ingenious and varied of all, particularly when passing from its first phase to the second; seen from close by, this can cause a powerful impression. The pedestals for sculptures were installed in 1746, and at that point it was intended to install four sculptural groups: *Cephalus and Procris*, *Bacchus and Ariadne*, *Zephyr and Flora*, and *Diana and Endymion*. However, the lead sculptures which we now see date from the first half of the 19th century and are based on classical prototypes.

The star shape of the **Ocho Calles** area is due to its original function as a hunting park, with a round central plaza and four secondary ones, all adorned with fountains after 1725.

Two pairs of fountains, those of **La Taza** ("the Cup") (F) on the upper line, and of the **Dragons,** also known as the **Tripod of Apollo,** (T) on the lower one, are placed as a landmark to detain the eye at the crossings of the avenues; they are almost identical except for slight nuances, such as the figures in the Taza Alta ("Upper Cup") being *tritons* while those in the Taza Baja ("Lower Cup") are *nymphs*; both were inspired by Giacomo della Porta's fountain in the Piazza Mattei in Rome, while those of the Dragons follow a design by Charles Le Brun. Among the groves of the Ocho Calles, worthy of note are the two large ones close to the Calle de la Medianería, known as the **Canal Groves,** which contain *cabinets de verdure*, prolonging the sequence of intimate spaces on the other side of this avenue, thus serving as a nexus between the

▲ *The goddess Latona asks Jupiter to transform the Lycian peasants into frogs. Fountain of Latona. Ocho Calles Sector.*

two principal different sectors of the garden. The groves, masses of trees delimited by the straight avenues of the garden, not only offer freshness and shade, but also create a contrast with the open parts. Those at La Granja consist of medium-sized trees surrounded by high hornbeam hedges, creating an effect of density inspired by French vegetation. In general, the interiors of the groves at La Granja were in a wild state: the predominant indigenous species, the oak, was allowed to grow to a maximum height of some twelve metres, so that its shade would not affect the growth of the linden and elm trees in the avenues. Since the late 19th century, the trees have not been pruned, and the large ones (particularly the conifers) are too tall.

The Plaza de las Ocho Calles is a scenographic success, though the slope means that the effect is not as fortunate as if it were at the highest point of the scheme, or on the flat. From its centre, occupied by the group of **Mercury carrying off Psyche,** it was possible at the same time to see the play of the four Cup and Dragon fountains, together with the eight occupying the areas between the avenues radiating from the plaza. These latter were built in 1734 and consist of basins with alternate straight and curved sides, formerly lined with marble and slate slabs in a chessboard pattern, and open arches which, standing out against the green background of the high hedges and the trees in the groves, contain eight statues of *Saturn, Minerva, Hercules, Ceres, Neptune, Victory, Mars* and *Cybele,* all by Frémin (though the first and last were completed by Dumandré), under arches of lead painted to resemble white marble

A Lycian peasant turning into a frog, Fountain of Latona. Ocho Calles Sector. ▲

and decorations of gilded bronze. Thus, a total of twelve *jeux d'eau* were visible from the pedestal of *Mercury carrying off Psyche*, counting those of the *Dragons* and the *Cups*, or even sixteen with those of the *Canastillo*, *Latona*, *The Three Graces* and *Fame*. The evening light reflected by the mountains is very beautiful in this plaza, from which one can walk down along the Calle Larga towards the Fountain of Latona; at the first cross avenue there are *four marble muses – Erato, Euterpe, Terpsichore* and *Thalia* – following models by Frémin but carved later by Bousseau. The same occurs with the other *five muses – Calliope, Clio, Melpomene, Polymnia* and *Urania* – and *Apollo* as if on Mt. Parnassus, in the other section of the Calle Larga, between the Plaza de las Ocho Calles and the Calle de la Medianería.

The **Fountain of Latona** was the penultimate one to be made. Around 1725 Marchand had the idea that the Calle Larga could terminate in a semi-circular labyrinth, adding further land to the garden. The new wall was already begun in 1728, though not in the imaginative form originally planned but limited to being a mere container of the main feature, which is the fountain, completed before 1737. Latona, who to flee from the vengeance of Juno wandered the world with her children Apollo and Diana, reaches Lycia and requests water from some peasants cutting reeds in a marsh; when they refuse, in irritation she calls on Jupiter for revenge, and immediately the miserable creatures are transformed into frogs: a very appropriate fable to refer to the difficulties of a sovereign during childhood, as occurred at

▲ *R. Frémin, J. Bousseau, P. Puthois and H. Dumandré: the Fountain of the Baths of Diana, 1737-45. Ocho Calles Sector.*

Versailles. Although to argue that such an intention existed here in relation to Isabella Farnese and her far from brilliant early position would be rather forcing the argument, it is certainly true that the mythological theme is of itself highly suitable to aquatic display: the *Lycians*, some already transformed into frogs and others in full metamorphosis, launch great jets of water like cries of stupor against the central structure, which becomes lost to sight in the paroxysm of the *jeux d'eau* playing in two very lovely phases.

The **Baths of Diana,** the last fountain made and the only one of an architectural nature, dates from the end of the reign of Philip V, as the ostentatious finishing touch of a garden of which the important hydraulic works at that time formed a homogeneous and closed unity. Its plan was by René Frémin and Jacques Bousseau, who were designing it in January 1737, and the definitive construction order was given on the 5th of October of the same year. The largest and best part of the sculpture is by Bousseau. Though the major work and basic water features were ready in 1743, it is believed that the overall composition was not fully completed until October 1745, by then under the supervision of Pierre Puthois and Hubert Dumandré. At the same time, the plaza was laid out with statues, benches and urns, the last of which were installed early in 1746. It is said that when Philip V saw it functioning for the first time, he said, "Three minutes you amuse me, and three millions you cost me."

Diana rests from hunting served by *five nymphs* present to wash, comb and dry her, while others, distributed around the basin, play with *dogs and dolphins* that spray jets of water into the air. Behind, in the midst of the architectural scenario of stone and marble, but as though hidden in a grotto (for the niche was originally decorated in this way, with *rocaille*,

René Frémin: Fame, mounted on the steed Pegasus *hurls a powerful jet of water to a height of over forty metres.* ▲
Fountain of Fame.

THE GARDENS

river pebbles, "conch and scallop shells, corals and other spoils from the sea, making up an attractive grotto"), a *faun* representing *Actaeon* plays the flute while espying the scene; the idyllic moment of this story has been chosen. Alternating with marble benches, four lead urns and *four hunting nymphs* by Puthois and Dumandré adorn the perimeter of the plaza.

All the area occupied by this fountain and plaza and by the Fountain of Latona is an addition (made between 1728 and 1737) to the original perimeter of the park, for when the Seat was created an iron gate stood here, through which the Monarchs entered on arriving from Valsaín and this gave its name to the avenue beginning opposite this fountain and leading to the Palace. The railing, by Sebastián de Flores, was moved, and constitutes the new gateway (of the Baths, or of Cosio) on the axis of Fame.

The **Grove of Fame,** against which the fountain giving its name to this whole design stands out, was planted with poplars at the end of the 18th century, but as conifers now predominate, the great height of the sculptural group does not dominate the scene as originally intended. *Fame*, mounted on the *steed Pegasus* and in the attitude of playing her trumpet, hurls her powerful jet of water skywards to a height of over forty metres, while several *Moorish soldiers* fall vanquished at her feet and down the rock, at the base of which are four figures representing the main Spanish rivers. This whole impressive "machine" (F), built around 1730, is influenced by creations of Bernini, but the main figure is directly inspired by a drawing of Charles Le Brun. The allegory refers not only to the role of the King as defender of the faith (alluding to the Christian conquest of the Islamic kingdoms of Spain), but also to the glory of Philip V as paladin of legitimacy both in the War of

Succession and in the various campaigns undertaken in those years in Italy, with the aim of providing states for his sons by Isabella Farnese; Charles finally obtained the Kingdom of Naples for Charles and the Duchy of Parma for Philip. At the entrance to the grove, in the plaza surrounding the oval pool, are two marble statues of *Lucretia* and *Atalanta* (F).

The **Parterre of Fame** was originally of the *compartiment* type, but in 1849 was remade as a *parterre à l'anglaise,* and in this form it has reached our times. When the Monarchs came to watch this fountain play, they occupied the area connecting the two pieces of lawn. The two marble sculptures represent *Apollo pursuing Daphne* (F) and were installed in 1730. The eight lead urns are among the finest in the garden: four show the arms of Philip V and Isabella Farnese (hers being the six *fleurs-de-lis*, not to be confused with the three of the Bourbons), while the other four have figures and hunting trophies taken from designs by Oppernord (F).

The Calle del Mallo, which forms the boundary of the parterre at its lowest point and separates it from the Grove of Melancholy and from the *Partida de la Reina*, was where the game of pall-mall, a sort of polo or croquet on horseback of which Philip V was so fond, was played.

Partida de la Reina is the name given to the gardens cultivated in the 18th century by Italian horticulturists, and to the old Pharmacy Garden. Beside its entrance is the Chapel of St Ildephonsus, to which the origin and name of this *Royal Seat* are due. Although Henry IV founded it in 1450, possibly as a votive offering to give thanks for deliverance from some incident relating to the hunt, from the outset it had the character of a lodge at which the king could rest during his days of hunting in Valsaín. It belonged to the Hieronymite monks of El Parral, who were given it by the Catholic Kings,

The Royal Collegiate Church and the old Casa de Damas, from the Medio Punto Gardens. ▶

remaining with them for 250 years until it was acquired by Philip V. Here the monks had one of their estates or "granges" like that of La Fresneda at El Escorial to which the members of this rigorous, aristocratic order could retire for periods of rest in the countryside. Though the site and area are those of the 15th century, the present construction dates from the 18th century, as in 1742 a gardeners' guild was founded and the King ceded this Chapel to it to serve as a headquarters. The next year they entirely rebuilt it to designs by Giacomo Bonavia, so that it was open again for worship by the summer of 1745.

Turning its back on these memories of the mediaeval royal hunts that took place here, the lively silhouette of the Bourbon Palace with its towers and south façade looks out onto the Parterre of Fame.

The Royal Palace and Collegiate Church

The Royal Palace of La Granja de San Ildefonso is a complicated building due to the successive interventions which contributed to its final form. Though constructed in a short time, it was extended and modified in response to the different functions it was required to perform, for though conceived originally as the place for the retirement of Philip V during his planned abdication, the "King Father's" return to the throne in 1724 meant that La Granja became the Sovereign's favourite residence and the *Royal Seat* for the summer "sojourn"; therefore, the building had to be enlarged following the patterns of European court architecture, and the dominant influence was the Queen's Italian taste. Those responsible for these later building campaigns were Italians: Procaccini and Juvarra, and their respective

disciples. In this way it evolved towards greater magnificence, the extensions and modifications to the Palace of San Ildefonso reflecting the progress of Italian taste in the Spanish court between 1720 and 1740.

Procaccini extended the Palace, creating four wings forming open courtyards to the north and south, and their construction took place between 1724 and 1734. At his death the problem had not yet been resolved of how to replace Ardemans' façade by another one which presided over and linked together the new Italian elements. This was the purpose of the façade designed by Filippo Juvarra in 1735, and built by his disciple Sacchetti from 1738 to 1741. When Juvarra's project was put into effect it had the result of altering the garden façade as conceived by Procaccini; his ideas for the central space corresponding to the Ardemans building were cancelled, and the side wings were altered. This change of plan, due both to Procaccini's death and to the greater prestige of Juvarra, meant that the grandiose central section of façade by Juvarra eventually dominated the areas to the sides, and led to the demolition of two of Ardemans' towers.

The intervention of Juvarra, responsible at San Ildefonso for this garden façade, the Monarchs' Bedroom and the (incomplete) gallery, is what gives the Palace of La Granja an obvious interest from the international point of view.

The ground-plan inside the rear cover shows how this process evolved. Before going inside the palace, we will take a look at the outside, as the most important façades look onto the garden.

The Architecture

The silhouettes of two towers, crowned by tall slate spires, and of the Chapel dome, easily visible from the Parterre of Fame, are the only

The façade of the Horseshoe Courtyard (Procaccini, 1735-41), in contrast with the towers of the original palace (Ardemans, 1720-23). Viewed from the Calle de Valsaín. ▶

features which give an idea of the original appearance of the Palace built by Ardemans between 1720 and 1723 for the King's retirement, and which was later hidden by the enlargements to the building that gave it its present aspect. Ardemans' palace was a curious variation on the traditional type of Hispanic Alcázar with four towers. In this regard, its peculiarity is that the towers were not at the corners, but rather inset within the building, which was square, with two floors and a slate roof. The central sections of the façades were slightly recessed, and painted to imitate brick, with the corners and surrounds of doors and windows in stone. To have an idea of its appearance one has to look at the two sections of the façade facing onto the Plaza de Palacio, on either side of the Collegiate Church.

The most characteristic and best-preserved feature of Ardemans' Palace is the **Fountain Courtyard,** in the centre of the building, surrounded by galleries over arcades which facilitated circulation. Around this there is a range of service buildings against which the towers are built, and all this is enveloped in the rooms of the outer range. The monumental staircase occupies the north range, and to the west is the Church.

As we noted above, Procaccini's extension resulted in both of the open courtyards situated between the four new wings. To the North, the **Carriage Courtyard,** which the visitor reaches from the Plaza de Palacio and opens onto the lower part of the gardens, was basically designed by the Italian architect, but the end façade reveals a mixture of elements

▲ *Teodoro Ardemans: The Fountain Courtyard.*

constructed at different periods: the main doors, like the staircase of honour which they open on to, are by Ardemans; the portico is by Procaccini, but corresponds to his two later designs, one of which refers only to the central arch, and the other to the rest, while the upper floor is Neo-Classical.

To the south, opposite the Parterre of Fame, is the **Horseshoe Courtyard,** which owes its name to its shape of a *cour d'honneur*, rare in Spain, opening out towards the Calle de Valsaín, since it was intended as the entrance for the Monarchs. The two structures to the left and right of the doorway are staircases, as revealed by the arrangement of their windows at different heights compared to the others. The one on the right led directly to the private rooms of Philip V and Isabella Farnese, and the one on the left to those of the Infantes. This courtyard, with its two rhythmically-arranged orders of composite order pilasters and columns, was undoubtedly the most attractive feature of the Palace until the arrival of Juvarra, and represents the last and most brilliant work of Procaccini as an architect: most of the construction took place after his death, being directed by his disciple Subisati. In the first phase, completed in 1735, the symmetrical staircase blocks and side galleries were built; and in the second (started in 1737, and concluded in 1741 by the stonemason Sánchez de la Barba) the gallery and façade at the end of the courtyard were constructed.

The lateral elements of the **east façade** are also the work of Procaccini, who here created a composition in which the forms of the late

The Axis of Fame, from the Fountain facing the Parterre and the Horseshoe Courtyard façade. ▲

Roman Baroque showed the influence of French Régence architecture. The arrangement of two superimposed orders and the complex rhythms of the Horseshoe Courtyard are retained, but enriched by a greater emphasis from the ends, where he used half columns on the ground floor, towards the centre of the wings, where he intended to place arcades of free-standing columns on the ground floor. These were to match another larger arcade planned by Procaccini for the centre of the façade facing the Cascade, to conceal Ardemans' original façade. However, Procaccini died in 1734, and Juvarra had very different ideas: the columns that were already installed were removed, and Sacchetti used them to decorate the atria of the Royal Palace in Madrid.

Juvarra's façade looking onto the parterre and the Cascade is one of the most admirable examples of late European Baroque architecture. Filippo Juvarra, who was summoned to Madrid to design the new Madrid Palace, arrived in March 1735, eight months after Procaccini's death, with his garden façade incomplete. The Monarchs decided to employ the new architect on this project also, commissioning him to design a central section to break the unity intended by Procaccini, as the ends of the wings he had designed seemed dramatically separate.

Juvarra's façade constitutes an autonomous unit proudly distinct from the sections to either side. It is articulated by means of pilasters and half giant columns of a composite order, very elegant due to the subtlety of their design and to the contrast between the pink Sepúlveda stone, the granite, and the Carrara marble in which the decorative sculpture is carved. The latter, by Baratta, represents the *Four Seasons* in the figures supporting the attic, and *Philip V as Mars and Isabella Farnese as Minerva* in the roundels. Also by Baratta are the capitals, the urns, the coat-of-arm, and the trophies of arms crowning the composition (as well as some other pieces which were not installed), but not the mascarons below the main balconies which are not of marble and are by Bousseau.

Its technical perfection and the gentle chromatic harmony of whites, grey, and pinks make this a magnificent façade; in its design it is heir to the European tradition of the two previous centuries, especially of the Italians, with marked echoes of Palladio, but also of the French and English.

However, as it was built it differs from Juvarra's design in fundamental aspects, since in reality it is an adaptation of the master's design, executed between 1737 and 1743 by Sacchetti, who had to deal with the difficult problem of scrupulously respecting the design, but adapting it to a very different programme, as he had to alter completely the ground-plan, levelling off the façade into one singe line. The mobile masses of Juvara's project, with one recessed area between two projections, corresponded to the royal wish to preserve the building of Ardemans, making it behind a

▲ *Filippo Juvarra: detail of composite pilasters and capitals.*

Central body of the façade, from the Fountain of Bacchus or of Autumn in the Palace Parterre. ▶

screen, without altering the interior or touching the walls, which would remain concealed behind a gigantic lining. As the new foundations adjoined the much weaker ones of Ardemans' Palace, they caused the ruin of the latter in 1736, after Juvarra's death. Accepting this situation, the Monarchs decided on the elimination of the pronounced recesses so that none of the projections could obstruct the view from the new central balconies.

Sacchetti thus not only built a screen-façade, but also, demolishing the entire former façade range, he built another entirely new and solid vaulted structure, with seven large rooms on each floor. Its façade followed Juvarra's plan, but altering the rhythm of the pilasters and the width of the axes so as to accommodate the straight-line sequence of the ground-plan, where projections and recesses are hardly more than insinuated, and eliminating the dramatic effect caused by the deep recessing of the windows with respect to the giant columns.

In homage to Juvarra and Sacchetti, two unused pilaster columns and some other marble ones which they commissioned were placed in the Fountain Courtyard.

In addition to the façade, Juvarra designed two further features for the interior of the San Ildefonso Palace: the Royal Bedroom, and the Gallery. This latter marks the end of the building efforts of Philip V in the Palace, just as the Fountain of Diana does in the gardens. In the following reigns, especially under Ferdinand VII and Isabella II, no further construction work was undertaken but the interiors were the subject of redecoration.

The Tour of the Palace

THE ROOMS of the Palace which are currently open to the public were the old royal apartments, located on the two floors overlooking the east façade opposite the Cascade. The main floor houses the Monarchs' private rooms, while the lower floor was used as a gallery to exhibit the Royal Collections. All the rooms (except those damaged in the fire of 1918) have ceilings with fresco paintings by the Italian artists Giacomo Bonavia, Bartolomeo Rusca and Felice Fedeli, with allegorical and mythological scenes framed by *trompe l'oeil* perspectives that open out the royal rooms onto the imaginary spaces of the Baroque.

The doors and windows are original, in walnut, olive, alder, and boxwood, made in different phases, the work carried out by Francisco Martín in 1735 being particularly outstanding.

The recent and painstaking restoration of these rooms has returned their interior decoration as far as possible to its original appearance during the period of Philip V.

From the Carriage Courtyard the visitor passes through the main gates on the south side of the Palace to the **Main Staircase (1),** designed by the architect Teodoro Ardemans, who adhered to the Spanish Baroque style in its conception.

The staircase consists of two lateral flights with a wrought-iron rail, above an archway with the entrance to the Fountain Courtyard, located within the central part of the old building. Above the doorway is a tapestry whose subject is the arrest of a poacher, and two hangings with coats-of-arms, all made in the 18th century in the Royal Santa Barbara Tapestry Factory by the master weaver Van der Goten.

Walking up the staircase the visitor reaches the rectangular **Room of the Halberdiers (2).** It has coupled pilasters and retains the original floor level of the old Palace; due to the difference in levels, a staircase leads up to the

Above, T. Ardemans: Main staircase. Below, lamp (left) and door (right) in the Royal Guard's Room.
Pages 48-49, the Axis of the Palace Parterre and New Cascade from the central balcony of the Monarchs' Bedroom. ▶

Royal Quarters on the left which consists of a series of rooms looking out onto the Cascade Parterre.

Opposite the doors which lead onto the gallery of the Fountain Courtyard and to the left is a large 18th-century chimney piece with firedogs.

The Main Floor Rooms

Room 3. The Royal Guard's Room. This small, square room functions as a crossing point, allowing access to the Royal Quarters through the Portrait Gallery and the Oratory, as well as to the Upper Gallery of the Fountain Courtyard. The ceiling still has a relief stucco decoration with a painted scene of Bellerophon killing the Chimaera (an allegory of the triumph of Virtue over Vice), by Bartolomeo Rusca. The Rococo consoles and the other decorative elements, the busts and the light, are

all 18th-century. After the death of Philip V, this room was used as an Oratory.

Room 4. The Portrait Gallery. This room was previously known as the *Tableware*, *Food* or *Serving Room*, indicating its previous function as an antechamber to the dining room. It was Isabella Farnese who had the decoration altered in 1760 to mark the first stay at the Palace of her son Charles after he became King of Spain. The room thus became the Portrait Gallery and the walls were hung with paintings of various members of the Royal Family.

The ceiling is painted with *trompe-l'oeil* architecture and depicts a gallery with a baluster rail, after a design by Bonavia, opening out in the centre with an allegorical scene of *Callisto transformed into the Great Bear* by Bartolomeo Rusca. On the left beside the door is a portrait of Charles III of Spain, King

▲ *Louis-Michel van Loo, 1737:* Philip V on horseback *(left);* Isabella Farnese *(right).* Portrait Gallery.

B. Rusca: Callisto transformed into the Great Bear, *fresco on the ceiling of the Portrait Gallery.* ▶

of the Two Sicilies by Giovanni delle Piane, known as Molinaretto. The sitter is depicted full-length wearing an elaborately embroidered frock coat and long waistcoat. The elaborate carved, wooden frame is dated 1732.

Various portraits flank the window which looks out to the main staircase: an equestrian portrait of Philip V and a portrait of Isabella Farnese in court dress, both by Louis-Michel van Loo and dated 1737; a portrait of the Infante *Don* Felipe, Duke of Parma, by Jean Ranc; and another of the Infanta Ana María Victoria, Queen of France, by Domenico Bradi.

Presiding over the room is the painting of *The Family of Philip V*, a copy of van Loo's original (now in the Prado), painted in the 19th century by Lozano Valle, and depicting all

the members of the King's family who were alive in 1742.

The room is furnished with 18th-century consoles and stools carved and gilded in the royal Spanish workshops. Worth noting are the clocks by Ferdinand Berthoud which were personally acquired by the King. The chandelier was made at the Royal Glass Factory of La Granja.

Room 5. The Small Dining Room. This room is also known as the *Stucco Decoration Room*. The ceiling was painted by Bartolomeo Rusca and depicts *Apollo killing the Serpent Python*. Painted within an oval medallion of curved outline against a background of sky is a representation of the story of Apollo (an allegory of Enlightenment). The god, leaning

▲ *The Small Dining Room.*

against the clouds, fires arrows (Rays of Light) at the serpent Python. In the upper part, the Hours guide the Chariot of the Sun, drawn by white horses. Around the central medallion are stucco rocaille decoration and six grisaille tondos with scenes of Apollo's feats.

Among the important pictures in the room are a number of still lifes by artists of various nationalities, including 17th-century *trompe-l'oeil* paintings by Franciscus Gysbrechts which depict an imitation pinewood wall with various weapons hung on it, and an open cupboard with papers and other objects. These highly realistic works were acquired by the Queen during her trip to Seville around 1733-1735. Two other *trompe-l'oeils* are also hung here, by Pedro de Acosta; the one on the right depicts a wall hung with

painting implements and prints, to the right of the balcony.

The allegorical paintings represent the five senses: *Hearing, Touch, Taste, Smell* and *Sight*, represented by women in different poses. They date from the 17th century and are by Abraham Janssens.

The furniture in the room consists of elaborately carved and gilded wooden chairs and stools in the Louis XV style made in the Spanish Royal Workshops. At the end of the room is an 18th-century dining table with a folding top, decorated with lemon wood inlay of bows.

Among the objects are two oriental porcelain flasks in the form of gods with a spout between the feet; these were originally used for pouring water.

18th-century chimney piece with its original grate, firedogs and pokers. The Dressing Room. ▲

The ceiling light was made in France in the 19th century.

Room 6. The Dressing Room. This room was at one point known as the *Chimney Piece Room*. Its smaller size meant that it had a more personal function than others in the Royal Quarters. The vaulted ceiling has stucco work decoration and painted decoration by Rusca depicting *Orpheus beaten by the Bacchants*. In the centre *Orpheus* appears above a mound holding a zither, clutched by the hair by a woman intent on beating him with a large stick, while other Thracian women pursue him. At the top lying among clouds, *Venus* looks on with two doves.

Above the chimney piece with its original grates, firedogs and pokers is a 19th-century carved wooden mirror. To either side are: paintings of *The Merry Drinker* and *Young Girl with a Biscuit* by Michel-Ange Houasse; the *Oath of Hannibal* by Jacopo Amigoni, of 1783; and by the same artist, *Don Carlos of Bourbon Crowned King of Naples*, of 1734.

The flower paintings are by the Flemish artist Jean Thielen and date from the 17th century. A large painting on the opposite wall depicts *Alexander defeating Darius* by Francesco Solimena; on either side are two grisaille battle scenes by Tempesta dating from the 17th century, and scenes with soldiers by Michel-Angel Houasse from the 18th century. Higher up are 18th-century landscapes by Frans van Bloemen.

The furniture includes carved wooden console tables based on a design by Juvarra and made by Bartolomeo Steccone. The room also contains pieces of oriental porcelain, bronze wall lights and a large crystal chandelier made in the Royal Glass Factory of La Granja by the master glassblower Juan Segismundo Scholze in the 18th century.

Room 7. The Oratory. This room was formerly known as the *Room where Mass is said*, and also the *Office*. The ceiling was painted by Bartolomeo Rusca and Giacomo Bonavia and represents the *Fall of Phaeton* in the central medallion. Among the clouds, *Phaeton* is depicted falling from *Apollo's chariot* which he has been driving. Above this we see *The Hours* with dragonfly wings, white tunics and red cloaks, raising their arms in a beseeching gesture. At the top on the right is a seated *Jupiter* in a gold crown and holding his thunderbolts, pointing imperiously down at *Phaeton*. To the sides of the god are the figures of *Juno and Hebe*.

The room also features an important collection of religious paintings, formerly belonging to the painter Carlo Maratta and acquired by the Monarchs in 1724.

Examining these from left to right we see: *Saint Anthony* and *Saint Joachim with the Virgin*, by Paolo de Matteis; *Saint Catherine*, by Maratta; *Saint Jerome*, by Mattia Pretti; a *Head of an Old Man*, by Sacchi; and *The Assumption of the Virgin*, by Carracci. Between the balconies are: an 18th-century marble tondo in relief depicting a saint; a *Penitent Magdalene* by Veronese, flanked by a *Mater Dolorosa* and *Saint Philip Neri*, by Carlo Maratta; a *Virgin and Child* by Carlo Cignani; a *Saint Barbara*, by Mattia Pretti; and a *Virgin and Child*, by Andrea Procaccini. On the other side of the door are: a *Saint Peter* by Luca Giordano of 1690; a *Saint Martha*, by Andrea Procaccini; and two interesting paintings on glass in the style of Luca Giordano representing *The Adoration of the Magi* and *The Adoration of the Shepherds*. To the right is a large painting of a historical subject depicting *Alexander the Great in the Temple of Jerusalem*, by Sebastiano Conca of 1737. Finally there is: a *Saint Jerome*, by an anonymous 17th-century Spanish artist; a *Saint Catherine* by

Sacchi; an *Infant Hercules sleeping*, by Simone Cantarini; *The Flight into Egypt*, by Giovanni Francesco Grimaldi; and *Saint Agatha* by Carlo Maratta.

The furniture in this room includes: carved and gilt wood console tables made in the Louis XIV style and dating from the first half of the 18th century; stools in the Louis XV style; and an important portable oratory which formerly belonged to Ferdinand VI with paintings by Andrés de la Calleja and an altar set with altar tablets and candlesticks made (*c.* 1826) at the Martínez Royal Silver Manufactory in Madrid, as well as a Louis XV-style stool in carved and gilded wood. The decoration of the room is completed by 18th-century oriental porcelain jars.

Room 8. The Monarchs' Bedroom. This room takes up the central area of the palace and lies on the axis formed by the New Cascade and the Collegiate Church. The ceiling was painted by Bartolomeo Rusca and depicts the *Marriage of Cupid and Psyche*, with *trompe-l'oeil* architecture by Giacomo Bonavia. The design of the ceiling imitates a rectangular gallery with concave and convex elements and a baluster rail and pedestals with vases of flowers. An Ionic colonnade supports an entablature crowned by another balustrade which acts as the background walls with an infinitely extended perspective. Above the four semi-circular arches on the main walls are oval medallions depicting *Psyche's amorous conquest of Cupid*. In the upper area are four further circular medallions painted in grisaille. The central allegory depicts Psyche dressed in blue and white above a cloud which is propelled by Zephyr and drawn by Mercury, who has wings at his head, feet and heels. He holds his caduceus in his right hand and has Hymen crowned with flowers at his feet, bearing the

The Monarchs' Bedroom. ▲

paintings depicting the *Magnificence of Alexander*, painted by Plácido Constanzi in 1737, and *Alexander before the Family of Darius*, by Francesco Trevisani and of the same year. These two paintings form part of a set of eight commissioned by Filippo Juvarra in 1735 for the *Salón de las Empresas del Rey* in the present building, and form part of the collection of Philip V. Also worthy of note are the paintings *Mark Antony and Cleopatra* and *The Vestal Virgin Tuccia*, by Andrea Casali, both of which came to Spain in 1736. Other religious paintings include a *Virgin and Child* by Carlo Maratta, and *The Ecstasy of Saint Francis* by Domenico Zampieri, known as Domenichino, as well as other religious works by anonymous artists. In the upper part of the balconies, in areas framed by rocaille work, are scenes of the *Labours of Hercules*.

The furniture comprises console tables in carved and gilt wood made in the 18th century by Steccone. On them are bronze figures of Apollo, Mercury and Cupid which are 17th-century copies of Hellenistic originals. The armchairs and stools were made in the Royal Workshops in the Louis XV style and are upholstered with a floral fabric. Among the decorative items are wall lights, cornucopias and vases and vessels of oriental porcelain from the Queen's Collection.

Room 9. The Queen's Room. This room was formerly known as the *Chimney Piece Room* or the *Square Room*. Originally, it housed part of Queen Isabella Farnese's major porcelain collection. It leads into the Room of the Spare Bed, which has recently been returned to its original form in the course of the recent restorations. The ceiling has an allegory of *the Triumphal Return of Jason and Medea*, framed with *trompe l'oeil* architecture by Giacomo Bonavia, imitating the upper floor of a covered

flame and repulsing Discord who is represented here with a head of serpents. At the lower right, seated on clouds, are Hercules, Minerva, Mars and other gods, who converse with each other. In the upper part, a winged, naked Cupid opens his arms and looks towards Psyche. He is accompanied by Venus, Pluto and Neptune and to his right are Jupiter, Juno and Hebe, together with other gods of Olympus surrounded by their *halo of immortality*. Higher up, the Hours throw flowers over the lovers.

The room is dominated by the bed with its imperial hangings in yellow damask, made in Italy in the last third of the 17th century, set with embroidery in silver thread over coloured silks in patterns of flowers and stalks forming scrolls, arranged geometrically. The hanging forms a canopy with seven festooned drops, embellished with silver fringing and topped with four urns. On either side of the bed are

▲ *18th-century chimney piece with its original trumeau, grate, firedogs and pokers. The Queen's Room.*

S. Bonavia: The Triumphal Return of Jason and Medea, *fresco on the ceiling of the Queen's Room.* ▶

courtyard with a curving balustrade on all four sides, with flags and military trophies in between. Each corner has an oculus with a balustrade extending into the space of the sky. One amusing detail is the man and woman painted in one of these oculi, looking down into the imaginary space of the courtyard. The whole composition opens out onto a panoramic sky in which we see Jason and Medea seated in a triumphal chariot pulled by white horses, surrounded by warriors, while Winged Victory gives Jason his prize and Fame goes ahead sounding a trumpet. In the lower right is a mother with a child in her lap watching the scene. In the upper part of the composition, two children with dragonfly wings (the Hours) witness the scene.

On the right, the room is dominated by a large composition of *Rebecca delivering the Jewels*, an anonymous 18th-century work probably by a follower of Amigoni. The paintings that decorate the walls are in a variety of genres: religious, allegorical and still life. They include *Saint Cecilia* by Guido Reni, the *Virgin of the Rosary*, by Artemisia Gentileschi, an *Allegory of the Liberal Arts*, by the 17th-century Flemish artist Martin de Vos, and scenes from the Old Testament like the *Judgment of Solomon*, by Pieter Aertsen of around 1562. Over the chimney piece are also flower paintings and still lifes by Jan Brueghel and Osias Beert dating from the 17th century. Also worth noting is the painting of *The Infant Christ with the Infant Saint John the Baptist served by Angels*, a work by the 17th-century artist Frans Synders.

The console tables are in carved and gilt wood and were made in the Royal Workshops in the 18th century, as were the Louis XV-style stools which complete the furnishing of this room. Above the chimney piece is a large mirror with a carved and gilt foliate trumeau topped by a coat of arms. Porcelain jars, *mille fiori*, cornucopias, wall lights and 18th-century firedogs complete the decoration.

Room 10. The Room of the Spare Bed. This room was also called the *Writing Room* or the *Room of the Reserve Bed*. Recently opened to visitors, it still retains its original wall painting depicting Diana at rest. In the centre of the ceiling is a rectangular scene of Diana after the hunt by Bartolomeo Rusca. Against a background of sky, the goddess is seen seated on rocks and accompanied by four seated nymphs with bow, arrows and quiver, while their dogs rest next to the spoils of the hunt. The room is dominated by a turned, wooden, Portuguese bed in the Manueline style of the 17th century. The walls of this room are hung with an important group of woven and embroidered pictures of religious subjects; particularly notable are those by Jacob Vandergoten the Younger and Andrea Rocchi, depicting the *Head of John the Baptist*, the *Archangel Gabriel* and *Salome*.

The furniture comprises a polychrome writing desk, a stool, a Louis XV table, bronze wall lights and other decorative elements of the same date.

Room 11. The Queen's Dressing Room. This room is also known as the *Room against the Tower*. It previously contained wood and stucco shelves displaying some 65 china figures of dogs, cockerels, children and other objects. The ceiling is decorated with stucco relief work and has a central scene of *Venus giving Arms to Aeneas* by Bartolomeo Rusca, surrounded by eight medallions in grisaille with scenes from the *Aeneid*. Aeneas, standing on a rocky outcrop, holds his lance in his left hand and points with his right towards Venus seated on the clouds who gives him the sword forged by

The Room of the Spare Bed. ▲

Vulcan. Other deities hold up the helmet as if about to place it on the hero's head, as well as the breastplate and shield. Behind the main scene, a group of warriors looks on.

Among the paintings which decorate this room are: a *Judith with the Head of Holofernes* and a *Bathsheba emerging from the Bath* by Francesco Solimena; an *Allegory of Ceres*, by Francesco de Mura, dated 1738; landscapes by Frans van Bloemen; and two views of the *Castel Sant'Angelo* and the *City of Viterbo* by Van Vitelli, both dating from the 18th century. Also worthy of mention are two small miniatures on board, the *Old Bagpipe Player* by the Flemish painter David Teniers II, and the

Group of Smokers by the Dutch painter Adriaen Brouwer, both 17th-century artists.

The furniture in this room is Baroque in style and consists of rich carved and gilded Louis XIV console tables, Louis XV stools, and a 19th-century French gilded bronze and glass lamp.

Room 12. The Queen's Ante-chamber. This area, which is also known as the *First Tiled Room*, originally consisted of six rooms that correspond with the south east wing of Procaccini's extended building. The name refers to the floor, which was originally tiled. All these rooms were damaged in the fire of 1918, when the richly decorated gilded stucco

▲ *Michel-Ange Houasse:* A Musical Evening, *in the Queen's Ante-chamber.*

and frescoed ceilings were destroyed, with the exception of the one in the first room, which depicts the Fall of Bellerophon.

The room is decorated with views of the Port of Naples by Giovanni Garro, and others of different ports, by the 18th-century Spanish painter Juan Ruiz. It also includes portraits and landscapes by 17th-century Flemish artists, and a large view of the Piazza Navona, painted jointly by Viviano Codazzi and Aniello Falcone. Certainly worthy of note are the paintings by Michel-Ange Houasse which depict a *School*, a *Musical Evening*, an *Interior Scene*, and *Villagers Playing under a Canopy*, as well as portraits by various artists.

The furniture comprises console tables in the Louis XV style in carved and gilt wood, by French makers of the second half of the 18th century, as well as stools with bombé legs.

The decorative objects include pieces of porcelain in blue and red colour schemes, cornucopias and clocks, all dating from the 18th century.

Room 13. The Landscape Room. This was formerly the site of the *Second Tiled Room*. The room's present name refers to the five landscape paintings that include scenes from Ovid's *Metamorphoses*, painted by Jacques d'Arthois in the 17th century. The furniture

B. Rusca, G. Bonavia and F. Fedeli: The Fall of Bellerophon, *fresco on the ceiling of the Queen's Ante-chamber.* ▲

consists of Fernandine Neo-Classical consoles and stools plus an original writing desk.

The vases on the tables were made in the Buen Retiro Royal Porcelain Manufactory and date from the reign of Charles III.

Room 14. The Old Oratory. This room was formerly the *Third Tiled Room*. Beside the door is a portrait of Charles III in hunting dress by Antonio Sebastiani da Caprarola. The King of the Two Sicilies has his right hand on the powder box and holds his gun in his left. To his side is a white dog.

On the entrance wall and on either side of the balcony are a collection of pastels depicting heads of saints and painted by Queen Isabella

Farnese in 1723. They surround a *Virgin and Child* by an anonymous 18th-century French artist. Other paintings include an *Armida and the Shepherds* by Ludovico Carracci and six small portraits of painters attributed to Van Dyck. Between them are Aubusson curtains dated 1867.

The console tables were made in the Royal Workshops in the 18th century. The mahogany stools date from the reign of Ferdinand VII and the decorative elements are of 19th-century French manufacture.

Room 15. The Dining Room. This was formerly Philip V's chamber, also known as the *Large Tiled Room*. The visitor can now admire

▲ *The Dining Room.*

F. Juvarra: mural decoration. Christ expelled from the Temple, *by Panini, in the central panel, marble dado, pilasters with* ▲ *oriental lacquers and carved and gilded ornamentation. Lacquer Room.*

the walls which, following a series of alterations, are covered with a modern, *grosgrain*, yellow silk. They are hung with a series of paintings of the parable of the Prodigal Son by Giuseppe Simonelli, dating from the 17th century. The canvases depict *The Prodigal Son Claims His Inheritance, The Debauchery of the Prodigal Son, The Flight of the Prodigal Son, The Prodigal Son Reduced to Poverty*, and *The Return and Pardon of the Prodigal Son*. Between the balconies are two Flemish landscapes by Jan Wildens. Above these are a *Country Picnic* by William van der Landon, and an *Annunciation to the Shepherds* by Bassano.

The furniture is in the Fernandine style and consists of a large table in Brazilian mahogany, console tables and armchairs covered in crimson brocatelle silk. Worth noting are the table decoration by the specialist in bronze work Pierre Philippe Thomire. The gilt and blued bronze ornamentation of the consoles and the clocks were made in French workshops during the period of the First Empire. The large gilt bronze and rock crystal lights are in the same style.

Room 16. The Lacquer Room. During the remodelling of the main garden façade, this room was the bedroom of Philip V and Isabella Farnese. It was designed by Filippo Juvarra and features oriental lacquer panels, paintings, carved decoration and different coloured marble. This combination of elements repeats a room designed by Juvarra in Turin and was extremely well received by the Queen. The carving in the room was executed by José Trul, Nicolás Argüelles and Andrés de la Viuda. The gilding was carried out by Sebastián Fernández and the marble dado is by Juan de la Calle and José Ris. The overdoors have paintings of *Christ and the Samaritan Woman* and *Christ on the*

Mount of Olives by Locatelli; on the walls are scenes of *Christ at the Probatic Pool, Christ Expelling the Merchants from the Temple, Christ Expelled from the Temple*, and *Christ Among the Doctors*, commissioned by Juvarra with Pannini, one of the leading artists in the genre of architectural scenes. The Monarchs' bed was previously situated in front of the balcony until the Queen ordered it removed to another bedroom and the lacquer panel now in its place installed.

This room was severely damaged in the fire of 1918, during which the ceiling paintings and the chandelier were destroyed.

Other elements in the room include a lacquered coffer and 18th-century oriental ceramics.

Room 17. The Mirror Room. Before the fire, the long walls of this room were embellished with mirrors with elaborate carved and gilt frames on a white background. The remainder of the room was faced with oriental red lacquer and decorated with 67 shelves displaying 150 china figures. The chimney piece, which was removed in the restorations of 1934, has now been replaced. The Mirror Room always had a musical function; in 1794 it contained a clavichord, and now has a piano by Pleyel. The fire totally destroyed the ceiling and the lacquered walls. Between the mirrors it is still possible to see remains of the red lacquer panels that survived the disaster.

The Walnut Staircase (18). The visitor reaches the ground floor via this staircase that was used only by Philip V and Isabella Farnese. It leads to the Horseshoe Courtyard where the rooms known as the "back quarters" and which were used as wardrobes were located between 1734 and 1743. The staircase has 18th-century carved and gilt wooden lamps

Pages 68-69, Filippo Juvarra: the Lacquer Room.

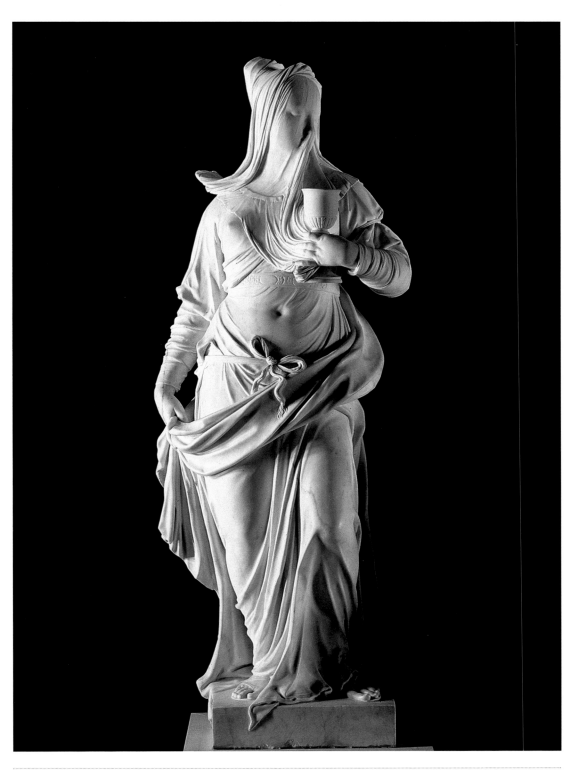

Antonio Corradini: Veiled Figure of Faith. *Room of Justice.* ▲

Pope Innocent XI. It was inherited by the Prince of Erba, who in turn decided to sell it.

Procaccini, court painter and artistic advisor to the Spanish monarchs, knew the collection well and advised Philip V to acquire it. In 1724 Cardinal Acquaviva was entrusted with the negotiations, and after some discussion, obtained it for a favourable price.

In 1725 the sculptures arrived at La Granja, where they remained in a rather haphazard state of arrangement until the death of Philip in 1746. After this date the collection was put into order by Isabella, who added some of her own sculptures. From 1789, Charles IV decided to send some of the sculptures to Madrid and Aranjuez, a decision that was mainly carried out by his son Ferdinand VII. In 1829, a significant group of what was left entered the Royal Museum of Sculpture and Painting, now the Museo del Prado.

Very few original sculptures now remain in the Palace of San Ildefonso. Some formed part of the King's Collection and are thus marked with the symbol of the cross of Burgundy, such as *Day and Night*, by Ercole Ferrata and the bust of Queen Maria Cristina, by Cartari, as well as a few other pieces now in Room 19. Also remaining in the Palace are some sculptures originally from the Queen's collection, notably Corradini's *Veiled Figure of Faith*.

Most of the sculptures now on display are plaster casts made in the late 18th century in the workshops at Valsaín and in those of the Royal Academy of San Fernando in Madrid. These casts are of particular interest as they were made before the restoration of the original sculptures and thus faithfully reflect the Collection as it was when installed by the Queen dowager after her husband's death in 1746.

From the inventory of 1766, made after the Queen's death, and from the description

and cornucopias on the side walls. In the niches are oriental vases and bronze figures of David sheathing his sword and of Venus, both painted in the 19th century by Antonin Mercié.

The Ground Floor Rooms

THE GROUND floor houses the sculpture collection of Philip V and Isabella Farnese. The collection was partly formed from sculptures which they inherited, but principally from their purchases of various 17th-century collections, such as that of the Marqués del Carpio, and most significantly, the collection assembled by Queen Christina of Sweden in the Palazzo Riario in Rome between 1653 and her death in 1689. The collection was sold by her heirs and was acquired by Livio Odescalchi, nephew of

▲ *Giulio Cartari:* bust of Queen Cristina of Sweden. *Room of Hercules.*

written by Antonio Ponz in 1787, we know where each sculpture was located. A reconstruction of the original layout of the gallery as it was in the 18th century before the rearrangements made in the 19th century has thus been possible.

The rooms which make up the sculpture gallery were decorated in the Italian manner, with stucco work, fictive architecture and allegorical ceiling paintings, executed by artists summoned by the Queen's Secretary, the Marqués de Scotti; among them were Giacomo Bonavia, who painted the fictive architecture; Bartolomeo Rusca, who painted the figures; and Felice Fedeli, who acted as assistant painter.

The inlaid polychrome marble floors follow the designs made by Bonavia during the last

years of Philip's reign but not carried out due to lack of funds. The stucco and marble walls add to the sensation of lightness and freshness in the room which helps it blend with the garden setting outside.

There now follows a description of the twelve rooms, which will be named after the subject of the principal allegorical painting on each ceiling.

19. The Room of Hercules. This room is located in the south east corner of the garden façade. Its ceiling has a perspectival architectural design painted by Fedeli following a design by Giacomo Bonavia. The architectural setting opens into a panoramic sky depicting a composition of The Strength of Spirit by Bartolomeo Rusca. The infant

J. Thierry: Fountain of Amphitrite bathing. S. Bonavia: wall frescoes. The Fountain of Galatea Room. ▲

Hercules in his cradle strangles two serpents with his bare hands. To one side, in a basket are his cloak and club. Alcmene, in a green cloak, approaches the hero, while Victory goes to crown him with laurel, bearing in one hand the staff of authority. From the peaks of Olympus, Jupiter, Juno and Hebe, with their respective attributes, contemplate the scene.

The room is dominated by a marble bust of Queen Christina of Sweden, carved by Giulio Cartari in the last quarter of the 17th century. Other portraits depict the Infanta Ana María Victoria, and Queen María Luisa of Orleans and her husband Louis I, painted by René Frémin. *Day and Night*, by the 17th-century artist Ercole Ferrata, the *Head of the Apollo Belvedere*, and a bust of Homer dating from the 17th century, complete the decoration of the room.

From this room is it possible to see the **Fountain of Galatea,** also called the Fountain of the Shells, designed by Jean Thierry, with the figure of Amphitrite bathing. It is located beneath the staircase in a small room **(20)** decorated in tempera by Bonavia in 1736. These are the oldest paintings to survive in the palace. The following rooms were all decorated between 1743 and 1746.

21. The Room of Valour. Also known as *The Small Room.* The ceiling is decorated with gilt stucco on a white background, creating traceries that frame the central painted scene of Valour crowned by Victory. Hercules appears seated among the clouds in a purple tunic, resting his left hand on the lion skin as a winged child approaches him. He looks towards Victory, represented as a winged maiden who approaches the hero to crown him with laurel. Recent restorations have revealed the stucco wall facings, while in addition to the sculpture of the goddess Flora, noteworthy is a

The Room of Victory. ▲

plaster cast of Ganymede, based on a 2nd-century Roman original and executed by Giuseppe Pagniucci *c.* 1797.

22. The Room of Victory. This room displays colossal statues which functioned as cult images incarnating divine power, here represented by casts of the original 1st- and 2nd-century sculptures. The ceiling is decorated with painted perspective settings, imitating a dado above the cornice with brackets, open oculi and medallions with winged children bearing military trophies, supporting the base of the four corners of a large gallery with a balustrade which opens onto a painted sky. In the centre is the Warrior, his helmet topped by a crest and a palm in his hand, while Victory approaches him, inviting him to appear before Glory who is represented higher up in the guise of a seated matron wearing a gold tiara and bearing a Pyramid (symbolising the glory of princes). Behind her, Time looks on. Fluttering about the sky are various infants bearing laurel wreaths and the Hoop of Immortality.

Presiding over the room is the figure of the god Apollo, flanked by two carved console tables on which are busts of Antoninus Pius and Caracalla. Between the windows opposite are the figures of the Emperors Augustus and Tiberius, made at the Royal Academy of San Fernando in 1797. The emperors are depicted full-length in cuirass and cloak. The head, legs and arms were gilded in imitation of the bronze of the original sculptures, while the bases are of interest as they belonged to the original sculptures. Notable are the reliefs on the front faces, representing Danaë and The Toilet of Venus, carved in marble by Pierre Etienne Monnot in 1693 and 1694 respectively. Other sculptures depict Jupiter Thunder, Poseidon, Tiberius in heroic nude pose, and

Augustus in a toga, all on pedestals with marble reliefs from the King's Collection.

23. The Room of Justice. The ceiling is of gilt stucco on a white background, framing a depiction of Justice and Reason of State, by Bartolomeo Rusca.

Displayed here is the sculpture of *The Veiled Figure of Faith*, executed in 1720 by Antonio Corradini, a gift from Cardinal Acquaviva to Isabella Farnese. It depicts a full-length female figure with the face totally covered by a veil. She holds a chalice in her left hand while her leg is bent in a gentle curve.

24. The Room of Peace. The ceiling is painted with a fictive architectural setting while the central medallion has a representation of an allegory of peace. Bellona admires Abundance (Ceres). In the lower part of the composition, the figure of War, in a laurel wreath, holds a lit torch.

Entering from the right is a sculpture of Hercules, after a 2nd-century copy of an original by Scopas. It formerly belonged to Queen Christina of Sweden, who had it completed with the addition of the legs and arms. This room contains other works by the cast maker Giuseppe Pagniucci: the *Young Bacchus* or *Satyr in Repose*, the Goddess of Abundance and *Ganymede giving a drink to Jupiter's Eagle*. The latter is based on Hellenistic prototypes, and the original is a Roman sculpture of the 2nd century, formerly in the collection of the Marqués de Carpio.

25. The Room of the Continents. Africa and America. The ceiling is decorated with gilt stucco and has a central oval medallion with a representation of Africa and America by Bartolomeo Rusca. Africa is depicted as a semi-nude black woman wearing a turban; in her

right hand she has a scorpion and in her left she holds a horn of plenty. She is accompanied by a lion and various snakes. America is represented as a naked woman with a headdress of feathers, holding an arrow in her right hand and a bow in her left. In each corner of the room is a medallion of curved outline with the figure of a winged child carrying the attributes of the two continents.

This room is also known as the *Room of the Reliefs*, referring to the original relief sculptures on display, such as: a *Saint Sebastian* by Matheo Clouet of 1770; a *Dog chasing a Wolf*, made in the Valsaín workshop in the first half of the 18th century; an anonymous 17th-century *Head of Christ*, based on a painting by Raphael; *Saint Charles Borromeo*, by an anonymous Italian artist of the 18th century; and an *Annunciation* by Hubert Dumandré dating from 1753.

On either side of the door are two lions rampant bearing cartouches by an anonymous Italian artist of the last third of the 17th century. Among the other sculptures in the room are figures of ephebes, Endymion (representing *Sleep* in the figure of a sleeping youth) and a *Faun with Kid*. Worth noting in the corner on the left among other sculptures is the figure of Narcissus, a cast after a Roman copy of an original by Polyclitus made around 410 BC.

B. Rusca, G. Bonavia and F. Fedeli: Allegory of Peace, Bellona admires Abundance. *Fresco on the ceiling, Room of Peace.* ▲

26. The Room of Europe and Asia. The ceiling has a fictive architectural setting with a central oval medallion depicting Europe and Asia seated on clouds. The perspective imitates a rectangular gallery with broken curvilinear pediments, balconies and large grisaille cartouches depicting the different parts of the world. Europe, in a gold crown, and Asia, in a floral crown, are accompanied by their symbols and emblems.

The small size of this room creates an intimate feel. In the absence of its original sculptures, small pieces from the Monarchs' Collection have been displayed here. They include a *Young Bacchus*, a *Faun playing the Panpipes* and *Polyhymnia*, made in the Valsaín workshops around 1797.

On an 18th-century gilt console table is a putto wearing a wreath of flowers by the 17th-century sculptor François Duquesnoy which previously belonged to the collection of Queen Isabella Farnese.

The decoration of the room is completed with a portrait of the Infante Felipe Pascual Antonio painted by Giuseppe Bonito in 1748.

27. The Marble Room or Room of Europa. The ceiling is decorated with stucco on a white background in the 18th-century style, while the central medallion represents the *Rape of Europa*. Jupiter, transformed into a white bull, carries off Europa on his back, dressed in white tunic and yellow cloak. Europa looks at her companions, who watch the scene in astonishment. In front of the throne, a woman holds out a garland of flowers, while on her left knee a child tries to pin one of Cupid's shafts onto the bull. In front of this retinue, a cupid bears Hymen's torch. In the upper part, winged infants attempt to shield the daring Cupid, covering him with a green curtain.

The Marble Room or Room of Europa. ▲

This room is richly decorated with various coloured marbles in the floor, and with the mirrors which follow a design by Sempronio Subisati, probably with the assistance of Giambattista Sacchetti.

On both sides of the doors are brackets bearing marble busts representing various Dianas and Roman emperors.

28. The Fountain Room. This is the central room in the façade, and corresponds with the axis of the Main Cascade and the dining room, with the exterior perspective extended into the interior by the presence of the fountain. It was originally proposed to decorate the walls with landscapes in order to integrate the room more closely with the garden, but this was never carried out.

In 1750 the fountain was altered and given its present form, increasing the size of the basin so that the water should not spoil the clay floor that Subisati had designed.

The ceiling is decorated with rocaille work, trophies and cornucopias of gilt stucco against a white background. In the centre, a rectangular medallion of curved outline has a representation of the *Rape of Persephone* by Rusca. In a rocky landscape, a nude, crowned Pluto bears Persephone in his arms towards his chariot with its white horses. Behind them, Ceres looks into the distance, while in the clouds two winged infants bear Cupid's quiver and arrows and Hymen's torch.

The room is presided over by a sculpture of Apollo by Francesco Maria Nocchieri, dating from 1680 (recovered in 2000 after its transfer by Charles IV in 1784 to the Prince's Garden in Aranjuez), and surrounded by the Muses Polyhymnia, Euterpe, Erato, Terpsichore, Urania, Clio, Calliope, and Thalia, executed in gesso by Giuseppe Pagniucci around 1792 and placed on the pedestals which held the original

Statues of Apollo surrounded by the Muses. The Fountain Room. ▲

sculptures before they were moved to the Royal Sculpture and Painting Museum.

On the consoles tables are busts of Antinoüs and Hercules, made in the Valsaín workshops in 1797 and at the Royal Academy of San Fernando, Madrid, respectively.

29. The Room of Truth. The ceiling is decorated with military trophies and victories in stucco against a white background surrounding the central medallion, in which an allegory of Truth, by Rusca, is represented. Time, depicted as an nude, winged old man, carries a nude young woman in his arms who represents Truth. To each side, winged infants bear the symbols of Immortality. In the lower part of the composition, seated on a cloud, is a female figure with a wooden leg, carrying a lighted bundle of straw and symbolising Mendacity.

This room features one of the most important sculptural groups from Queen Christina's collection and the most famous sculpture at the Palace of La Granja: the so-called *St Ildephonsus Group*. From an early date, the figures were identified as Castor and Pollux offering a sacrifice to the goddess Persephone, evoking the pain of separation when the first died and the second ascended to the heavens. The original group dates from the 1st century AD. This is now in the Prado Museum and the present group is a cast by Giuseppe Pagniucci of 1792, but the base is original; worth noting on it is a 2nd-century marble relief representing a battle between barbarians and Romans, formerly in the collection of Queen Christina of Sweden. In the upper right corner is a cross of Burgundy, which identifies it as having been in the King's Collection.

Equally worthy of note are the *Satyr Resting* and the *Jupiter Thunder*, which are based on 2nd-century AD prototypes.

30. The Room of Venus. The ceiling has a fictive perspective with oculi closed by balustrades and brackets supporting the oval which opens into a panoramic sky in which we see Venus asking Vulcan for the arms which he has forged for Aeneas.

On a pedestal is the reclining figure of Clytia on some rocks, semi-nude with crossed legs, her left hand held up and her right turning into a heliotrope, a plant which turns towards the sun during the course of the day. The original sculpture is a Roman fragment (the lower part of a nymph's torso dating from 100 BC), while the torso, head, arms and feet were made around 1675 by Giulio Cartari. On show here is the cast made by Pagniucci around 1795 which shows the sculpture as it was when it was in the Royal Collection before it left La Granja.

31. The Conquest Room. Above the cornice from which the ceiling vault springs is a painted fictive architectural setting that opens onto the sky. A circular medallion is painted with an Allegory of Conquest by Bartolomeo Rusca. In the centre of the composition is a bearded old man seated on clouds and wearing a purple tunic. His right arm is covered by armour and he holds a sceptre in his hand. With his left hand he holds up a laurel wreath which he is about to place on the head of a woman seated at his feet. To her side we see a bull's head, while in front two winged infants hold up an open book and two more approach with another weighty tome.

The room also contains *Venus with a dolphin*, a sculptural group of an athlete with an amorino, probably representing Faun or Paris, made in the Valsaín workshops around 1797. In the inventory of Queen Christina of Sweden's collection there is a reference to a "nude man with a child", which must refer to a

Giuseppe Pagniucci: cast of the St Ildephonsus Group, *1792. The Room of Truth.* ▲

Monarchy as compared to Versailles; one might even see an echo of El Escorial in the view from the Puerta de Segovia, although this was not the Monarchs' original point of access, which was the Calle de Valsaín. Ardemans built a Chapel with a ground-plan in the shape of a Latin cross characteristic of the Madrid Baroque style, with an elegant dome completed on the 19th of September 1723. The interior was articulated by a Doric order of pilasters, converted into Ionic with rich decoration of garlands and sculptural elements in stucco, following a design of Sabatini in 1766. At that time Bayeu and Maella painted the ceiling frescoes, but due to the fire of 1918 and another fire in the lantern of the dome in 1945, all that remains are *The Four Evangelists* in the triangular pendentives, by Bayeu.

The High Altar was designed by Ardemans, with a wealth of richly coloured marble (red from Cabra, white and green from Granada) and bronzes, though not all of the latter cast for this purpose were installed. During his last years, Ardemans dedicated all his attention to this project. The painting is an important work by the Neapolitan artist Francesco Solimena. It features *The Holy Trinity and the Virgin adored by Saints Philip, Elizabeth, Louis of France, Ferdinand, Charles Borromeo, Antony and Teresa of Jesus*, all patron saints of different members of the Royal Family; painted after 1730, it replaced a similar work by Procaccini that is now in the parish church of El Rosario and is well worth visiting.

The Royal Gallery, facing the High Altar, was also designed by Ardemans, though built under the direction of Román, who took charge of its installation and gilding early in 1725. The marble columns supporting it were brought from Rome with the sculptures of Queen Christina of Sweden. Below, the choir stalls were carved in 1724 by the woodcarver Juan Panadero. In the nave are urns portraying Our

sculpture made up of fragments of various Roman pieces.

The Collegiate Church

FROM THE Plaza de Palacio the visitor reaches the Royal Collegiate Church of the Holy Trinity, formerly the Palace Chapel.

Philip V wished to dignify it with this rank in order to give greater splendour to the worship in his place of retirement, endowing it with a Chapter headed by an Abbot who was a prelate *in partibus*, with unlimited jurisdiction independent of the Bishop of Segovia over the Royal Seat and its dependencies.

The position of the Chapel on the axis of the entrance to the Seat has been stressed as a differentiating factor of the Spanish Catholic

▲ *Teodoro Ardemans: the high altar in the Royal Collegiate Church.*

Teodoro Ardemans: the Royal Gallery above the Choir. Royal Collegiate Church. ▲

Lady of the Rosary and Our Lady of Sorrows. On the side altars, also dating from the changes made by Sabatini, are two large canvasses: *The Bestowal of the Chasuble on St Ildephonsus* by Procaccini, and *The Immaculate Conception* by Maella.

Reached via the door on the left in the Sanctuary, the Relics Chapel was consecrated as such in 1735, but after the death of Philip V the decision was taken to convert it into a Royal Pantheon, and for this purpose it received further decorative elements. The Funerary Monument of Philip V and Isabella Farnese, facing the relics altar, was built following a design commissioned in Rome; the plans arrived late in 1748, and early the following year Puthois and Dumandré stipulated the types of Spanish marble with which it was to be built. Thus, the design must be by Ferdinando Fuga, and the presumed intervention of Subisati would be limited to adapting the design to its site, since it seems to have been intended for a more spacious setting. Regarding the marble sculptures, *Charity*, *Fame* and the *Medallion of Isabella Farnese* are by Dumandré, and the remainder by Puthois, including those supporting the royal coat-of-arms. The stuccoes are by Sermini. Opposite, the *Triumphant Christ*, a stucco relief by Luis Salvador Carmona, surmounts the *Reliquary* (urns by Chavarría and Trevisani, 1729, and Nicolás Argüelles, 1735), beneath which the Infanta Isabel (known as *la Chata*, "Snub-nose") was buried in 1990. The ceiling painting is by Francesco Sasso. The provisional sepulchre (1746-1758) of Philip V is behind the High Altar of the Collegiate Church, in an intermediate room separating it from the Sacristy, above which is the Chapter House.

The façade of the Collegiate Church towards the Plaza corresponds to this block of Sacristy and towers, added following a design by Procaccini, assisted by Subisati who directed the works. It is clearly inspired by Italian, late-Baroque works, and, ultimately, by the apses of St Peter's in Rome by Michelangelo. The two side porticoes of the Church were also designed by Procaccini and were built at the same time as the upper parts of the towers, in 1727, by the same craftsmen: the stonemason Andrés Collado and the stone carver Diego de Arce, who also created the nearby Fuente del Mallo (Pall-Mall Fountain), in a picturesque corner close to the Plaza de Palacio.

Back in the Plaza, the visitor may like to complete the visit with a walk around the little town of San Ildefonso, which has the double appeal of its well-preserved 18th-century architecture and noteworthy local cuisine.

The Tapestry Museum

THE TAPESTRY Museum occupies a purpose-built wing constructed in accordance with a project by Miguel Durán (1932) on part of the site of the old *Casa de Oficios*, later the *Casa de Damas* (which from the reign of Charles IV until they were completely destroyed by fire in 1918 contained the private rooms of the monarchs) returning to the idea of creating a permanent display of these tapestries, already suggested in 1899 (to be next to the Royal Armoury of Madrid) and again in 1926 (in Aranjuez), as hitherto they had been seen only rarely and then incompletely when hung in the gallery of the Madrid Palace for important official events.

The Tapestry Collection of the Spanish Crown, the richest in the world together with that of Vienna, owes its exceptional quality and quantity to the dominion of the Spanish Sovereigns of the House of Austria over the Low Countries, principal producer of this

F. Fuga and Subisati: the Cenotaph of Philip V and Isabella Farnese. The Relics Chapel, Royal Collegiate Church. ▶

refined art form. The taste for the tapestries of Flanders had already taken firm root in late-mediaeval Spain, fitting in well with the Mudéjar tradition of moveable applied decoration, easily transportable and capable of transforming any space into a rich room when, furthermore, the court had no fixed seat. Thus, by the end of the 15th century, large quantities of tapestries were to be found in the homes of the higher ranks of the aristocracy and the Catholic Monarchs, and this taste continued to flourish during the 16th century under Charles V and Philip II. Only the break in the political links of Spain with Flanders, as a consequence of the War of the Spanish Succession at the beginning of the 18th century, brought an end to this supply of tapestries, and Philip V decided to create the Royal Tapestry Factory of Madrid, which still survives. Though the greatest number of pieces and those of the best quality in the collection are in these rooms, very many

more are to be found in the other Royal Palaces (particularly those of Madrid, El Escorial and El Pardo), and on deposit in embassies and official buildings. Mention will be made, if not of all, at least of the principal series exhibited here.

The Honours, by the Brussels weaver Pierre van Aelst from cartoons attributed to different artists (mainly Van Orley and Gossaert de Mabuse), consists of nine allegorical tapestries, four referring to personal ethics *(Fortune, Prudence, Divine Wisdom* and *Faith)*, four to public ethics *(Fame, Justice, Nobility* and *Infamy)*, and one, *Honour,* representing the culmination of this moral discourse applicable to the young Emperor Charles of Habsburg, crowned in 1520, the year appearing in *Fortune.*

The series was finished in 1523, but was not sent to Charles V until 1526, when he was in Seville. The programme was established with great precision by an anonymous but erudite person who is represented on the extreme right

▲ *W. Pannemaker and J. Gheteels:* St Michael defeating the Devil, *tapestry V in the* Apocalypse *series. Tapestry Museum.*

of *Infamy*, and it has been presumed that he is Jean Lemaire des Belges.

The ideas are based on authors of antiquity like Ovid and Valerius Maximus, and on humanists like Boccaccio, Petrarch and Alain de Lille; they are given concrete form as figures from ancient and mediaeval history, and allegorical personifications, each identified with its name. To follow the programme sequentially, the tapestry of *Honour* should be imagined in the centre, at the far end of the room, with the tapestries relating to personal morality to the left, and those on public morality to the right.

The Apocalypse consists of eight tapestries woven before 1561 for Philip II by Willem Pannemaker and Jan Gheteels, from cartoons attributed to Van Orley.

Other 16th-century tapestries exhibited on this floor are *The Labours of Hercules*, by Gheteels, and three panels of *The Fables of Ovid*, by Pannemaker.

On the ground floor, the series of *The Creation of Man*, from cartoons by Michael Coxcie, was woven in the 17th century by Fobert and Vervoert. *The Triumphs of Petrarch* (of *Love*, of *Chastity*, of *Death*, of *Fame* and of *Time*) are based on the poems from that series, and were woven from cartoons also attributed to Van Orley.

The Royal Woodland and Palace of Riofrío

LEAVING SAN Ildefonso in the direction of Segovia, and soon after passing the bridge over the River Eresma there is a turning to the left with the old garden of Robledo on the same side, created for Charles IV when he was Prince of Asturias. The road climbs until one can enjoy a panoramic view over the entire Royal Seat of La Granja, and continues

surrounded by *dehesas* (wooded pasture land) and meadows that make it very pleasant, until after twelve kilometres it comes to an end at one of the gateways in the high stone wall surrounding seven hundred hectares of woodland of holm oaks, deciduous oaks, junipers and ash trees, where a large number of fallow deer may be seen grazing. In the centre is a pink, square, 18th-century Italian palace. This is Riofrío.

However, as this gateway *(Puerta de Castellanos)* is usually closed, one has to leave the local road at the crossing with the main highway, continue towards Madrid, and then take a turning that is signposted further on, to the right. The visitor thus enters the Royal Wood by its main gate, the *Puerta de Madrid*. Another entrance, the *Puerta de Hontoria* (or *de Segovia* because it leads to that city, nine kilometres away), is also open from eight in the morning until sunset.

The main entrance to the Palace of Riofrío. ▲

Riofrío was a grazing pasture and hunting reserve which Philip V rented from 1724 onwards. The estate greatly pleased the monarchs for their hunting expeditions, but its sale to the *Real Patrimonio* was obstructed by the fact that it belonged to the *mayorazgo* (entailed estate) of the Marqués de Paredes, who was legally unable to dispose of it.

When Philip V died in 1746, the widowed Queen had the use of San Ildefonso for life, but it nevertheless remained Crown property. Proud as she was, and on poor terms with her stepson Ferdinand VI and his wife Barbara de Bragança, Isabella Farnese feared that the possible presence of the royal couple in La Granja would relegate her to the background, and she therefore wished to create a little court-city that would depend on her alone; she loved hunting, money was not a problem and she liked building, and so arose the idea of turning the hunting reserve into a *Royal Seat* which, according to Teresa Lavalle, could later have been used as a residence for the Infante Louis, younger son of the Dowager Queen.

Ferdinand VI approved of his stepmother building a second residence, as this would virtually remove her from La Granja, and he granted two complementary favours: a permit allowing the sale of the property, and a decree of total jurisdiction for the distinguished new owner. The purchase was finalized on 19th of July 1751, and on the 25th of the same month the King granted his stepmother full civil and criminal jurisdiction over her estate as mistress of the place. Subsequently, Queen Isabella increased the size of the property by acquiring other neighbouring land on the basis of purchase and exchange. Further additions were made during the reigns of Charles IV and Isabella II, and the result is a hunting woodland that was unaffected by the sales of properties of the *Real Patrimonio* in the 19th century.

However, the buildings that were to have made up the Royal Seat – barracks for the Spanish and Walloon Guards, stables, accommodation for court employees, a Franciscan friary and a theatre, in addition to gardens to be laid out in the French style by Champion – remained at the design stage. Of these, all that was actually built was the wing

The main façade of the Palace of Riofrío from the Casa de Oficios. ▲

that has always served as *Casa de Oficios* (staff
accommodation); the curve of its light,
harmonious façade frames the block of the
Palace, which gracefully raises its Italian
silhouette against the Castilian sky. The
integration of the Palace into the woodland
could not be more fortunate, though caused not
by deliberate landscaping but rather by a chance

political-dynastic reverse: Ferdinand VI died
without ever visiting La Granja and Queen
Barbara pre-deceased him. In 1759, aware of
the impending arrival of her son Charles III, the
Queen rushed to Madrid, and paid no further
attention to Riofrío. Later Monarchs used
the Palace exclusively as an oversized hunting
lodge, leaving it otherwise empty and untended.

It was only during the reign of Isabella II and the Restoration that it was used by two monarchs for extended periods: *Don* Francisco de Asís used it during trips to La Granja in the last years of Isabella's reign, and above all, Alfonso XII used it when in mourning for his first wife, Mercedes de Orléans.

Both monarchs had minor decorative improvements carried out, as the basic solidity of the structure made major restoration work unnecessary. The royal apartments were hung at the end of the 19th century with a large number of paintings which were later transferred to other palaces.

The Royal Palace of Riofrío

THE PALACE, which gives a singular air to this hunting park, evokes the proud figure of Isabella Farnese, incapable of accepting a secondary role, rich, splendid and untroubled as to the wisdom of her building projects. However, it does not reflect her aesthetic tastes, but rather those of her secretary, Marquis Annibale Scotti, who intervened several times in the royal works, finding fault with the architects in charge of them, particularly Sacchetti at La Granja and Madrid, and favouring Bonavia. His severe criticism in 1741 of Sacchetti's project for the *New Royal Palace* of Madrid, which was then under construction, led to consultation by the Spanish court with the prestigious Roman architects Fuga, Salvi and Vanvitelli, who drew up a major report on the Palace. A comparison between the Palace of Riofrío and the ideas then expressed by the Queen's secretary on what a royal palace should be reveals that Riofrío was the work of Scotti: ten years after his attacks on

▲ *The Main Courtyard of the Palace of Riofrío.*

One of the two stairwells of the Main Staircase of the Palace of Riofrío. ▶

the Master Architect, when in 1751 the Queen decided to construct her own new Royal Seat, Scotti's architectural concepts were realised, albeit posthumously, as the project was put out to tender on the 18th of May 1752 and Scotti had died three months earlier. The contract was signed on the 1st of July 1752 with a group of Italian architects headed by Andrea Rusca and Bartolomeo Reale. The foundation stone was laid on the 24th of October 1752 and work continued under the direction of Rabaglio only until February 1753, then under Carlo Fraschina until his death in 1757, Pietro Sermini and José Díaz Gamones. It was concluded in 1759, though work on details continued until 1762. All the original plans are now in the Royal Academy of San Fernando in Madrid.

The Palace of Riofrío is square, each side being 84 metres long, and its height is approximately 24 metres. Each side of the central courtyard is 32 metres long. Compared to the Madrid Palace, it takes account of the criticisms directed against the latter by Scotti: the courtyard was enlarged at the expense of the building, and the exterior simplified by eliminating the columns, pilasters and mezzanine floors. The symmetry is more accentuated than in Madrid, as the four façades have the same projections, the courtyard occupies the exact centre of the ground-plan, and its two axes coincide with the entrances. In Madrid, the arrangement of two double staircases facing each other and the situation of the Chapel, not in the entrance range but in the opposite one on the far side of the courtyard, were suggestions by Scotti which Sacchetti followed in every detail in July 1742. Thus, the three fundamental features of the interior of Riofrío – the staircases, the courtyard and the chapel – are a reflection of what the Madrid Palace should have been according to Scotti.

The staircases face each other on either side of the main vestibule, producing a theatrical effect inspired by Juvarra. They are both of the Imperial type, and the stairwell is articulated with a light, elegant Corinthian order. The stone balustrades, following a design attributed to Jacques Marquet, are decorated with allegorical groups of figures of children sculpted by Joaquim Dumandré and André Bertrand.

The Courtyard, built entirely of carved granite, and with the entrances marking the Palace's double axes of symmetry, is closely based on the Main Courtyard of the Madrid Palace, as there also it was intended to divide the arches of the main gallery into balcony and skylight.

The Chapel, on the side opposite the staircase, as imposed by Scotti in Madrid, has here the advantage of occupying only the inner range on this side, without interrupting the flow of apartments or being apparent from the outside. It is elliptical in shape and the altar is on the lower floor. The royal gallery is on the upper floor, above that of the Palace servants, a logical arrangement in a place not intended to be the setting for court ceremonial. The original marble floor is preserved. Above the altar is a *Virgin and Child with Saints Barbara and Francis of Sales*, attributed to Antonio González Ruiz. In the sacristy, where there is a marble basin, and in the vestry rooms, there are several originals and copies, including a crucifix by Sacchi and a *Coronation of the Virgin* on glass by Giordano.

In the 1960s, part of the main floor was set aside for a Hunting Museum, a project developed by the Marqués de Lozoya with the collaboration of Ángel Oliveras and Ramón Andrada; the display was basically didactic in approach and included reproductions of antique weapons, paintings of hunting subjects and tableaux of stuffed animals created by the taxidermist Benedito and the set designer Emilio Ruiz del Río.

The Bedroom of Alfonso XII. ▶

Bibliography

General

Ponz, Antonio: *Viaje de España*, Vol. XI, Madrid, 1787.

Martín Sedeño, Santos: *Compendio histórico, topográfico y mitológico de los jardines y fuentes del Real Sitio de San Ildefonso, Colegiata y fábricas y la de los Reales Sitios de Valsaín y Riofrío...* Madrid, 1825. Successive editions, 1831; expanded by Andrés Gómez de Somorrostro: 1845, 1852, 1854, 1861, 1867.

Fagoaga, José de, and Muñico, Tomás: *Descripción de los Reales Sitios de San Ildefonso, Valsaín y Riofrío...* Segovia, 1845.

Breñosa, Rafael and Castellarnau, Joaquín María de: *Guía y descripción del Real Sitio de San Ildefonso.* Madrid, 1884. Facsimile ed. Biblioteca Nueva-Icaro, La Granja, 1991.

Bottineau, Yves: *L'art de cour dans l'Espagne de Philippe V*. Bordeaux, 1962. Spanish ed. Fundación Universitaria, Madrid, 1986. Revised and extended ed., Sceaux, 1992.

Bottineau, Yves: *L'art de cour dans l'Espagne des Lumières*. De Boccard. Paris, 1986.

Contreras y López de Ayala, Juan de, Marqués de Lozoya: *Palacio Real de La Granja de San Ildefonso*, Patrimonio Nacional. Various editions, the 8th corrected and augmented by Concha Herrero Carretero, Madrid, 1985.

Morá Turina, Miguel: *La imagen del rey. Felipe V y el Arte*. Nerea, Madrid, 1990.

Lavalle, Teresa: *La obra de Andrea Procaccini en España*. Academia, 73 (1991), pp. 381-398.

Lavalle, Teresa: *El mecenazgo artístico de Isabel de Farnesio, reina de España*. Unpublished doctoral thesis, Universidad Autónoma de Madrid, 1994.

Sancho, José Luis: *La arquitectura de los Sitios Reales. Catálogo histórico de los Palacios, jardines y Patronatos Reales del Patrimonio Nacional*. Patrimonio Nacional-Fundación Tabacalera, Madrid, 1995.

Reales Sitios, magazine of Patrimonio Nacional from 1963 onwards.

Callejo Delgado, María Jesús: *Real Sitio de La Granja de San Ildefonso*. Lunwerg, Madrid, 1996.

El Real Sitio de La Granja de San Ildefonso. Retrato y Escena del Rey. Exhibition catalogue. Madrid, 2000.

Sancho, José Luis: *Las Vistas de los Sitios Reales por Fernando Brambilla. La Granja de San Ildefonso*. Doce Calles, Madrid, 2000.

The Gardens

Dézallier d'Argenville, J.A.: *La théorie et la practique du jardinage*. Paris, 1713. Well-known 18th-century manual.

Winthuysen, Xavier de: *Jardines clásicos de España*. Madrid, 1930. Facsimile ed. coord. by Carmen Añón, Doce Calles, Madrid, 1989.

Digard, Jeanne: *Les jardins de La Granja et leurs sculptures décoratives*. Paris, 1934.

Casa-Valdés, Marquesa de: *Jardines de España*. Espasa-Calpe. Madrid, 1982, pp. 153-165.

Morán Turina, Miguel: "El Rapto de Psique. Felipe V y los jardines de La Granja", *Fragmentos*, no. 6 (1985), pp. 39-44.

Var. Auth.: *Otoño en los jardines de La Granja*. Madrid, 1990.

SANCHO, José Luis: "Los jardines de La Granja de San Ildefonso", *Reales Sitios*, No. 120 (1994), pp. 17-28.

Los jardines de La Granja de San Ildefonso. Doce Calles, Madrid, 2001.

The Royal Palace

KUBLER, George: "Arquitectura de los siglos XVII y XVIII", in *Ars Hispaniae*, Vol. XIV. Madrid, 1957.

BATTISTI, Eugenio: "Juvarra a San Ildefonso", in *Commentarii*. Bologna, 1958, pp. 273 et seq.

IRANZO FERNÁNDEZ, Rita: "El Palacio de La Granja. Tradición e innovación en las residencias reales españolas de los Austrias a los Borbones". *Punto y Línea* (Valladolid), nos. 7-8, 1989, pp. 17-32.

MARTÍN, Pompeyo: *Las pinturas de las bóvedas del Palacio Real de San Ildefonso*. Patrimonio Nacional, Madrid, 1989.

GRITELLA, Gianfranco: *Juvarra. L'Architettura*. Modena, 1993.

ORTEGA VIDAL, Javier, and SANCHO, José Luis: "Entre Juvarra y Sacchetti: el emblema oriental de La Granja de San Ildefonso", *Reales Sitios*, no. 119 (1994), pp. 55-64.

Filippo Juvarra. Exhibition catalogue, Madrid, 1994.

JUNQUERA DE VEGA, Paulina, and HERRERO CARRETERO, Concha: *Catálogo de Tapices del Patrimonio Nacional. Vol. I: siglo XVI*. Patrimonio Nacional, Madrid, 1986.

JUNQUERA DE VEGA, Paulina, and DÍAZ GALLEGOS, Carmen: *Catálogo de Tapices del Patrimonio Nacional. Vol. II: siglo XVII*. Patrimonio Nacional, Madrid, 1986.

HERRERO CARRETERO, Concha, *Catálogo de Tapices del Patrimonio Nacional. Vol III: siglo XVIII. Reinado de Felipe V*. Patrimonio Nacional, Madrid, 2000.

MARTÍN, Fernando A.: *Catálogo de la Plata del Patrimonio Nacional*. Patrimonio Nacional, Madrid, 1987.

COLÓN DE CARVAJAL, José Ramón: *Catálogo de Relojes del Patrimonio Nacional*. Patrimonio Nacional, Madrid, 1987.

SÁNCHEZ HERNÁNDEZ, María Leticia: *Catálogo de Porcelana y Cerámica española del Patrimonio Nacional en los Palacios Reales*. Patrimonio Nacional, Madrid, 1989.

PASTOR REY DE VIÑAS, Paloma: *Historia de la Real Fábrica de Cristales de San Ildefonso durante la época de la Ilustración (1727-1810)*. Fundación Centro Nacional del Vidrio-CSIC-Patrimonio Nacional, Madrid, 1994.

Riofrío

See General Bibliography, and also:

RUIZ ALCÓN, María Teresa: "El Palacio de Riofrío", *Archivo Español del Arte*, XXXVI (1963), pp. 281-296.

HERRERO, María Jesús: *Palacio de Riofrío (Guide)*, Patrimonio Nacional, 1990

Arquitecturas y ornamentos barrocos. Los Rabaglio y el arte cortesano del siglo XVIII en Madrid. Real Academia de Bellas Artes de San Fernando, Madrid, 1997.

The printing of this book, published by Patrimonio Nacional, was finished on the 5th of Junio, 2014, at Artes Gráficas Palermo

REAL SITIO DE LA GRANJA DE SAN ILDEFONSO
THE ROYAL PALACE AND GARDENS

A CARRIAGE COURTYARD. Visitors' entrance
B PLAZA DE PALACIO. Entrance to the Royal Collegiate Church
C TERRACE AND HORSHESHOE COURTYARD. Entrance Gate to Gardens
D FOUNTAIN COURTYARD
E ARCO DEL INFANTE ARCH. Book and Gift Shop
F PALACE PARTERRE TERRACE
G MEDIO PUNTO GARDENS

MAIN FLOOR
1 Main Staircase
2 The Room of the Halberdiers
3 The Royal Guard's Room
4 The Portrait Gallery
5 The Small Dining Room
6 The Dressing Room
7 The Oratory
8 The Monarchs' Bedroom
9 The Queen's Room
10 The Room of the Spare Bed
11 The Queen's Dressing Room
12 The Queen's Ante-chamber
13 The Landscape Room
14 The Old Oratory
15 The Dining Room
16 The Lacquer Room
17 The Mirror Room
18 The Walnut Staircase

GROUND FLOOR
18 The Walnut Staircase
19 The Room of Hercules
20 The Fountain of Galatea Room
21 The Room of Valour
22 The Room of Victory
23 The Room of Justice

24 The Room of Peace
25 The Room of Africa and America
26 The Room of Europe and Asia
27 The Marble Room or Room of Europa
28 The Fountain Room
29 The Room of Truth
30 The Room of Venus
31 The Conquest Room
32 Connecting Room
33 Book and Gift Shop
34 Exit to Gardens and Carriage Courtyard

TAPESTRY MUSEUM
35 Main Floor. Ground Floor (exit)

ROYAL COLLEGIATE CHURCH. PALACE CHAPEL
36 Atrium
37 Presbytery
38 Choir and Royal Gallery
39 Relics Chapel. Philip V and Isabella Farnese Cenotaph
40 Provisional resting place of Philip V (1746-58)*
41 Sacristy*
42 Chapter House (Main Floor)*

(*) not open to the public

Animals
and Their
Travels

MIGRATIONS FROM ONE REGION TO ANOTHER

by RICHARD A. MARTIN

Illustrated with Photographs

Maps by Ray Pioch

REVISED EDITION 1961

GOLDEN PRESS

NEW YORK

Library of Congress Catalog Number 61-16938

The Earth and Its Animals

About a million different kinds of animals live on the surface of the earth, on land and in the seas. But animals do not live just anywhere in the world. Each kind lives naturally in a particular kind of place. This natural living place is called the animal's habitat. In its habitat, an animal must find all the things that are necessary to its way of life. There must be the right amounts of air and water, of heat and light. The air or water pressure must be just right; and there must, of course, be suitable food for the animal. As they grow up, some animals change their habitats. Toads and dragonflies, for instance, live the early part of their lives in the water and the latter part on land.

Some parts of the world are crowded with animals. In a few places there are none at all. And once having found a suitable place to live, animals do not always stay there. To understand why animals live where they do and how they move about over the earth, it helps to know about the different kinds of climate and vegetation on the earth.

Climate is mostly a matter of temperature and rainfall. The tropics re-

Penguins could not live in woods nor could butterflies live in the cold of Antarctica.

7

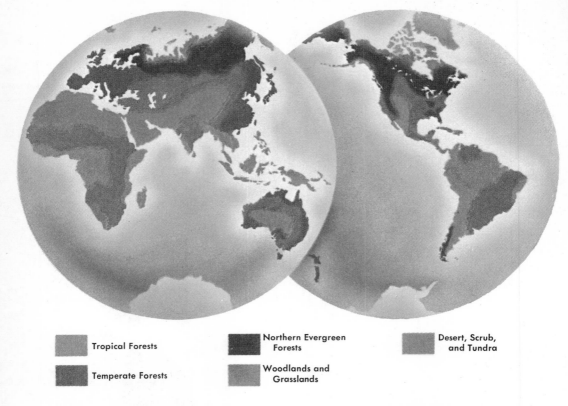

As this map shows, different types of vegetation grow in uneven bands around the earth.

Tropical Forests

Temperate Forests

Northern Evergreen Forests

Woodlands and Grasslands

Desert, Scrub, and Tundra

ceive so much heat from the sun that they are hot all year round. The polar regions get so little heat even in summer that they are almost always cold. The amount of rainfall a region gets depends on winds. Water vapor picked up by winds blowing over the ocean and other wet places is carried to regions where it condenses and falls as rain. In general, the tropics have a great deal of rain because of winds that blow into them from high pressure bands at their edges. Most of the world's deserts lie in these bands of high pressure north and south of the tropics.

From the poles to the equator, the number and kinds of plants that grow vary with the climate. Below the region of permanent ice and snow at the North Pole where no plants can grow at all, there are tundras—regions where the plants are small and scanty. Tundra gives way to the northern evergreen forests. Farther south, the evergreen forests are replaced by temperate forests of trees that drop their leaves in winter. The temperate forests in turn give way to the tropical rain forests.

Within these general zones there are many regional variations. Ocean currents, distance from the sea, and mountains all affect the local climate and vegetation. Even a simple diagram shows that vegetation zones are not even, uniform bands around the earth.

Less than a third of the earth's surface is land. All the rest is sea. Living in the sea is much more the same everywhere than is living on land. Probably no part of the great ocean habitat is without its animals. But the regions in which the tiny floating plants (that are part of the sea "soup" called plankton) are most abundant usually contain the most animals.

The movement of animals over the earth is sometimes called migration. To most people the word means the annual journeys that birds make in the spring and in the fall. There are, however, other animals that may move with the seasons.

Eels, elephants, bats and turtles are among the animals that migrate with the seasons. Migration can also mean the natural spreading out of an animal into new territory. In this sense all animals migrate. The word is used for still other kinds of animal travels, too.

Some kinds of migration are movements of great masses of animals traveling long distances together. Others are short, unnoticed journeys of individuals. Some are active on the part of the animal that is migrating. Some are passive—that is, the animal itself has nothing to do with its journey, but is, in some way, carried along. Some migrations are disastrous for the migrating animals, but most kinds are beneficial. Almost all types of migration tend to spread the many different kinds of animals over an ever greater part of the earth's surface.

Migrating south in the fall, Canada geese escape the winter cold.
They fly north again in spring to their breeding grounds in Canada.

Flying brown bat

Garter snake

Carp

Barn owl

Red squirrel

Norway rat. Of mammals, only man and some bats are more widespread than rats.

10

Normal Migration

A pair of red foxes ordinarily has a family of five to nine puppies a year. If all of the puppies grew up and stayed close to their parents, and if each of the young foxes had puppies every year that also stayed nearby and had families of their own, in time there wouldn't be enough food in the neighborhood for all of the foxes. But as soon as they are able to take care of themselves, most young animals wander off. Gradually, the area occupied by an animal may get bigger. Such spreading is called normal migration.

In normal migration the travels of animals are not easy to see, and often the journeys are short. The spreading out may be so slow that only over hundreds or thousands of years is there any obvious change in an animal's range. It is, however, the most important kind of migration for establishing an animal in new regions. It is slow enough to permit the animal to adapt itself to new conditions.

If there is nothing to stop it, an animal may spread widely over the earth. The thistle butterfly has done so. So has the osprey. The sperm whale and the thresher shark are among the animals which are at home in every ocean.

But not many of the earth's animals are so widespread. Barriers are often in the way. The sea, of course, is a barrier to land animals just as land is a barrier to animals of the sea.

Australia is now separated from all other land by oceans. Except for bats and some rodents, none of the big group of mammals that spread over other continents have ever crossed the ocean barrier to Australia on their own. The unusual mammals, such as the koala on this page, which are native to Australia are thought to be descendants of a few egg-laying and pouched mammals that reached that island continent millions of years ago, perhaps by way of land bridges joining it to other parts of the world.

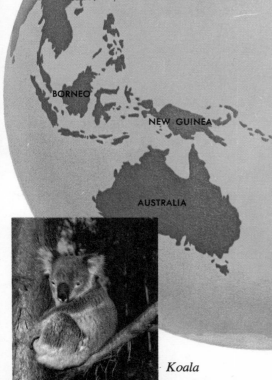

ASIA

BORNEO

NEW GUINEA

AUSTRALIA

Koala

11

Accidental Migration

A volcanic explosion killed almost all life on Krakatoa, but soon plants, insects and, finally, animals reappeared on the island.

In 1883 Krakatoa, a small volcanic island east of Java in the South Pacific, blew up. The only part of the island which was left above sea level was buried under a thick layer of ash. Nothing was left alive on the island except, perhaps, one kind of earthworm. In time, however, plants began to grow again. And 14 years after the explosion there were spiders and flies, bugs and beetles, and butterflies and moths living there.

By 1928, 45 years after the disaster, a great many kinds of animals made their home on Krakatoa. In addition to insects and other kinds of very small animals, there were land snails, birds, bats, rats, lizards, one kind of crocodile, and one kind of snake. The nearest land was almost 12 miles away. How did all these animals get to Krakatoa? The birds and bats, and perhaps some of the insects, could easily fly the 12 miles over the ocean. The crocodile and the snake could swim the distance. Probably most of the small animals were carried to the island by winds. The lizards and the rats perhaps floated there on pieces of driftwood. The snails could have traveled to Krakatoa either on the wind or on waterborne coconuts or on driftwood rafts.

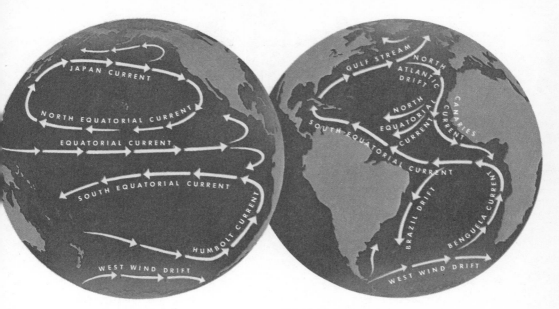

Even some land animals can be carried to far regions by ocean currents.

The travels of the animals that came to Krakatoa by wind and by rafting are examples of accidental migration. Throughout the ages many kinds of animals have been carried to new regions in similar ways. There are records of rains of fishes after tornadoes. Animals such as snails, frogs, and salamanders can be carried away in hurricane winds and dropped miles from where they were picked up.

In rafting, ocean currents may play a part. Driftwood, floating coconuts, or masses of detached seaweed may ride long distances on ocean currents carrying small animals with them. Floating "islands" of earth tangled with bushes and grass may be washed out to sea from flooding rivers and carried far away on ocean currents. Even animals larger than rats and lizards might travel to new regions on such drifting "islands" and become established far from their original home.

Some of the most widely distributed animals in the world are among the tiny floaters and drifters that ride the ocean currents as part of plankton. Many of the larger animals that live in the sea are small enough in their early stages to be part of plankton. Then they, too, are carried far and wide in the sea by currents.

But in most cases, traveling by chance is not a very important part of the story of animal migration. Many of the animals carried by wind and wave and raft die without ever reaching a haven and establishing themselves in a new region.

13

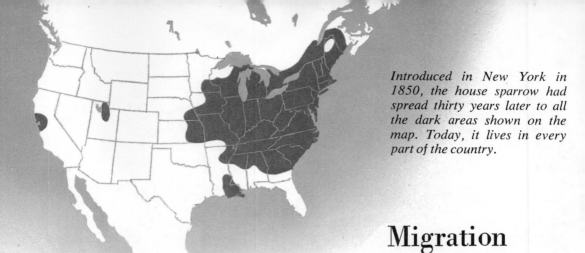

Introduced in New York in 1850, the house sparrow had spread thirty years later to all the dark areas shown on the map. Today, it lives in every part of the country.

Migration through Man

Rabbits live in parts of every continent except Antarctica. But until about 100 years ago no rabbit had reached Australia. Rabbits did not get to that island continent until people took them there. Rabbits are good food, and hunting them is good sport. Some of the English people who settled in Australia decided to stock the land with rabbits from their homeland.

In 1859, two dozen rabbits arrived in Australia and were set free. The rabbits did well in their new home. There was plenty of food for them, and they had no natural enemies to prey on them. They even found burrows made to order. Those of one of the bandicoots (rat-like pouched animals) were exactly right for European rabbits. The rabbits forced the bandicoots out and used their burrows as nests for their own families.

In a few years there were thousands of rabbits; then there were millions. The rabbits became a terrible plague.

They ate the crops and stripped the grazing lands. The Australians brought in foxes to prey on the rabbits, and they killed as many of the rabbits as they could. The government helped in the fight against rabbits. Australia began shipping rabbit meat, rabbit fur, and felt made from rabbit fur to the rest of the world. But all the money made from the rabbits could not make up for the damage already done.

For thousands of years people have helped animals to spread into new regions. They have helped some animals on purpose, just as they helped to establish rabbits in Australia. They have taken others with them as they traveled with no thought of spreading the animals in new places. They have carried many unknowingly. Barnacles have traveled long distances on the bottoms of boats. Rats have sailed all over the world as stowaways. Some of our worst insect pests came to America in cargoes from other lands.

14

Animals that have been carried along as food or as pets have become established in places far from their original territory. A kind of frog now living in marshes in England is thought to have been brought there from Italy during the Middle Ages. The Italian monks who established the frog in Britain used it as food. Turtles and snakes are among the other animals that have been carried about by travelers as food or as pets.

The famous Barbary "ape" that lives on Gibraltar is the only macaque (a kind of monkey) found west of Pakistan. One guess as to how it got to Gibraltar is that Arabs brought some of these "apes" with them as pets when they conquered the Spanish peninsula many hundreds of years ago.

Two birds brought by men to the United States on purpose are the common house sparrow and the ring-necked pheasant. People who had known the sparrow in Europe thought that it would be a help in controlling insect pests. But the bird spread so rapidly that it has crowded out other birds that eat many more insects than it does. It has now become a nuisance everywhere in North America.

The ring-necked pheasant of Asia was freed in America in 1881. It, too, found its new home to be a good one. Now it is common in fields and farmlands over much of the United States. Unlike the house sparrow, however, this bird has not interfered with other native birds and has not become a nuisance. It is one of the favorite game birds. It is so well liked that thousands are raised every year by conservation agencies and then released.

Before introducing an animal into a new region, people should be as sure as possible that the benefits will outweigh any disadvantages. The story of the house sparrow shows how serious such an introduction can be. But the story of the pheasant points out that not all animal introductions to new lands have proven to be unwise.

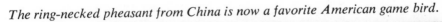

The ring-necked pheasant from China is now a favorite American game bird.

Occasionally, locusts reproduce in huge numbers and migrate on long flights.

Sporadic Migration

One of the ten plagues in Egypt, as the Old Testament relates, was a plague of locusts. The locusts "covered the face of the whole earth, so that the land was darkened; and they did eat every herb of the land . . . and there remained not any green thing . . . through all the land of Egypt." Later, as the Bible story tells, a mighty west wind blew all the locusts out of Egypt and into the sea.

Ever since the dawn of history there have been locust plagues like the one in Egypt in many different parts of the world. The grasshoppers which are called locusts are common in dry, grassy regions. Every now and then moisture conditions are exactly right for grasshoppers and these insects hatch in great numbers.

In such years, the grasshoppers that hatch do not grow up to be exactly like grasshoppers of ordinary years. They are a little different in color, size, and shape. And they are much more active. The young ones gather in masses and move out from their overcrowded home ground stripping plants of their leaves as they go. The grasshoppers take to the air when they grow up and get their wings and they make long flights to regions far from their breeding grounds. It was once estimated that a vast cloud of grasshoppers migrating over the Red Sea covered an area of 2,000 square miles.

The Norwegian lemming is a mammal that now and then spills over from its native territory. In most years this little hamster-like rodent stays quietly at home in the highlands of Norway. But every few years, lemmings begin to multiply very fast. Soon their land is unbearably crowded. The lemmings begin to move in droves down the mountainsides into the valleys. For months they push on, multiplying as they travel. Hawks, owls, foxes, and weasels follow and feed on them. Many are drowned or trampled along the way. Others die of exhaustion and starvation. None of the lemmings that migrate ever return to their mountain home, and none ever succeed in establishing permanent lemming colonies in the lowlands.

Collared lemmings migrate much as Norway lemmings do but their mass suicidal migrations are somewhat less spectacular.

Pallas's sand grouse is a bird of Central Asia that, probably because of overcrowding, has occasionally appeared in Europe in great numbers during the past 100 years. There, hundreds of miles from its home in Asia, it settled in sandy hills along the coasts as far west as the British Isles. But at no time was the bird successful in establishing itself permanently in Europe.

The travels of the locusts, the lemmings, and the sand grouse are examples of what is called sporadic migration. "Sporadic" means "now and then." Overcrowding, or overpopulation, is a common cause of sporadic outbursts of many kinds of animals into new regions. Sometimes such migrations do bring about extension of an animal's range, but more often they end in disaster for the migrating animals. Sporadic migration does, however, make conditions better for the animals that stay at home.

Periodic Migration

Such journeys as those made each year by birds between two regions are called "periodic migration." In periodic migration there is always a return trip to the place from which an animal starts. Often the travels are repeated each year at certain seasons. Some round-trip journeys, however, are made only once in the lifetime of an animal.

Many animals made periodic migrations long before birds did. Even before there were any birds, some of the invertebrates of ancient seas must have made seasonal journeys to lay their eggs in safer places, to find better supplies of food, or to find water of the right temperature.

Along the eastern coast of North America there is a creature with a very old pedigree, the horseshoe crab. It is the only survivor of a once widespread group of animals. The horseshoe crab

For millions of years horseshoe crabs have moved in to shore each spring to lay their eggs in the sand at the ocean's edge. The crabs then return to the sea.

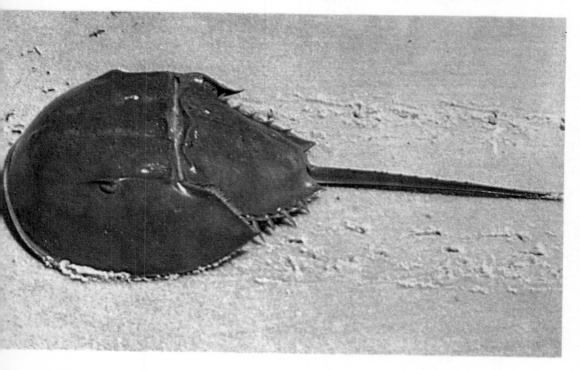

has lived in the ocean almost unchanged since the early days of dinosaurs. It shared ancient seas with many animals that have been gone from the earth for millions and millions of years. And every spring since it first appeared in the sea, the horseshoe crab has moved in toward shore. There it scoops out hollows for its eggs in the sand between the marks of the tide. After laying its eggs it leaves them to hatch in the sun-warmed sand and moves back into deeper water. This annual journey of the horseshoe crab may be the oldest periodic migration still made today.

Many of the horseshoe crab's more modern relatives also move about in the sea in accordance with the seasons. The lobster and the blue crab move from shallow water in summer to deeper water in winter. Shrimp, too, migrate between the coastal regions and distant deep water. Shrimp fishermen must know where and when to look for shrimp if they are to bring back good hauls. In order to find out more about where and when shrimp travel, scientists tag some of the shrimp or mark them with dyes of different colors and put them back in the sea. Careful records are kept of where these shrimp are picked up.

Some invertebrates that have adapted themselves to living on land reverse the horseshoe crab's egg-laying journey. The fiddler crabs that spend their year burrowing in the dry beach sand along the coast move down to the water's edge in spring carrying their eggs on the underside of their bodies. As the eggs hatch, the baby crabs are flipped into the water. Young crabs must live and grow up in the sea. In the West Indies, where some land crabs live a mile or more inland, the annual trip to the ocean is wonderful to watch. Great numbers of these crustaceans gather and crawl off to the sea in one long, wide parade of crabs.

The Republic of Cameroon, in Africa, got its name from the Portuguese word for "shrimp." Every spring tiny shrimp-like crustaceans swim from the sea to rivers to lay their eggs.

19

Ladybird beetles, or ladybugs, like many other insects, make short journeys to protected places to hibernate for the winter.

Insects

The commonest of all the animals of the earth are insects. Insects like the grasshopper with good strong wings can fly long distances. You might expect them, then, to migrate north and south as birds do. Yet extensive periodic migration is almost unknown even among the strongest flying insects.

In regions where winters are cold, some insects may make short migrations to hibernate in safe hiding places. A ladybird beetle may travel from the garden into the kitchen and spend the winter there, hidden in some tiny crack. Other kinds of ladybirds may make longer journeys at the end of the summer. Often ladybirds gather in big groups and hibernate together under leaves and logs. In the West, some ladybirds migrate in the fall to places high in the mountains, where they gather in great masses and hibernate throughout winter. A hibernating cluster may be several inches deep.

Ladybirds are good friends of farmers and fruit growers because they eat so many aphids and scale insects that damage crops. People in the West often gather the hibernating beetles by the sackful and store them until they are needed in the growing season.

The monarch butterfly is a famous insect migrant. Toward the end of summer these pretty butterflies, common almost everywhere, gather in flocks and fly south. The butterflies travel in long, thin lines on sunny days in the fall. They stop at night to rest and may stay several days in one place before they travel on. In their leisurely journey south, some of these butterflies travel several hundred miles. When they reach their winter resort in California or along the Gulf, the monarchs settle on trees. There they spend the wintertime in a dormant state. Year after year, the monarchs travel to the same "butterfly trees" to hibernate. In spring the monarchs move northward one by one, but only the females travel very far. After they have laid their eggs, they die. The monarchs that people see in summer are not the butterflies that flew south the year before. They are another generation.

There are other butterflies that migrate, but we know less about their habits than we know about the habits of the monarch. Among the other migrating butterflies are the little sulphur butterfly and the painted lady. The little sulphur is known to fly in great swarms across the Caribbean Sea to the Bermudas.

The monarch butterfly is an insect that does make mass migrations south in the fall, just as many birds do. In the spring, the whole colony moves northward again.

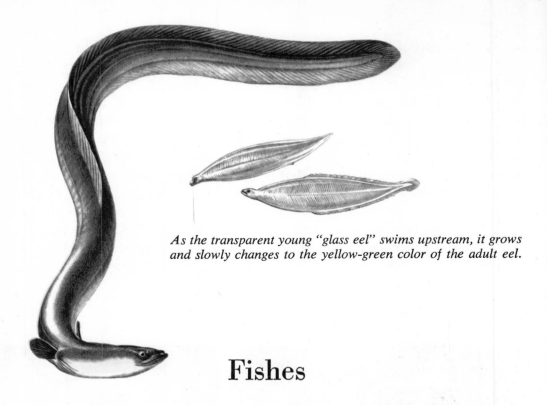

As the transparent young "glass eel" swims upstream, it grows and slowly changes to the yellow-green color of the adult eel.

Fishes

Some fishes can live only in fresh water, some can live only in the sea, and still others can live in both fresh and salt water. The fresh-water eel is one that can live in both. It is common in many streams and rivers in Europe and eastern North America, as well as in some other parts of the world. But part of its life it spends in the ocean. Only recently have scientists learned about the long trip made by this eel.

Every fall, adult eels swim downstream to the sea. European eels head westward to lay their eggs, or spawn, in one small area of the calm Sargasso Sea in the Atlantic between Bermuda and the West Indies. Some of the eels may have to travel 5,000 miles to get

there. American eels swim toward the same general area, but their journey is not so long. African eels swim to the Madagascar Deep. No one yet knows where some of the other fresh-water eels go to lay their eggs.

Eels are strong swimmers, but it takes them several months to reach the spawning area where the eggs are laid and fertilized in early spring. One female eel may lay as many as 20 million eggs. From the time they begin their migration to the sea, eels eat nothing at all. It is believed that they die after the eggs are laid.

The eggs soon hatch into flat, transparent creatures about one-quarter of an inch long. The new-born eels, or

Below, *in the waters of a tributary stream salmon lay their eggs. The eggs hatch over the winter and the fish swim downstream the following spring.*

Salmon may have to jump up falls and over rapids as they fight their way up a swift river to their spawning areas.

Salmon may swim 2,000 miles upstream.

larvae, begin a slow, drifting journey back over the hundreds or thousands of miles of ocean which their parents crossed before them. They eat and grow as they travel. In the coastal waters near shore they change greatly in looks. They lose their flat shape and begin to grow fins. But they are still transparent. In this stage they are called "glass eels."

The little glass eels swim along the coast until they find a stream. The females swim upstream. There, they live and grow for many years until it is their turn to cross the sea and lay eggs in the far-off breeding area. Male eels

23

stay and grow up near the shore, in bays and in the mouths of rivers. When the females move downstream and head for the sea, the males join them and migrate with them.

Many puzzling things happen in the life cycle of the fresh-water eel. No one knows why the tiny larvae of the European eel drift eastward toward Europe and those of the American eel move toward the west from their common hatching ground in the Atlantic. No one knows, either, how the tiny creatures find their way. But the greatest mystery of all is why the adult eels travel to such a faraway part of the sea to this one area to lay their eggs.

Of all migrant fishes none is more famous for its periodic travels than the Pacific salmon. Each year, from March

A weir in Alaska traps migrating fish.

through the summer, salmon pour inland from the Pacific Ocean to spawn in rivers and streams along the west coast. King salmon may swim a thousand miles upstream in the Columbia River and two thousand miles in the

Another danger for migrating salmon are such animals as this brown bear.

Yukon. Dangers of all sorts beset them throughout their trip up the rivers. Fishermen watch for them with hooks and nets and traps. Bears, eagles, and ospreys prey on them. There are steep falls and turbulent rapids to hurdle. All the way the salmon must fight swift river currents.

Today, great dams that block the way are additional hazards in western rivers. In spite of fish lifts and ladders salmon are lost in tremendous numbers at dams. By autumn, the fish that overcome all obstacles and escape their enemies have now reached the end of their journey. There, in the gravelly bed of a tributary stream, the eggs are laid and fertilized. So far as anyone knows, no king salmon live to go back down the river to the ocean.

By the next spring, the little fish that have hatched from the eggs start downstream to the sea. A great many of them, too, are lost along the way. After a few years in the ocean, when they weigh an average of 25 pounds, king salmon swim in toward the coast, search out the mouth of the river which they themselves came down, and begin their inland journey. Often they go on to the very stream where they were hatched. No one knows for sure how the fish pick out the right river to enter

At some dams there are fish ladders that permit migrating salmon to pass around the dam and continue up the river. Each step up the ladder is a deep pool of water.

or how they can trace their way to one certain tributary stream. Many scientists think that the salmon find their home river and birth stream through their very keen sense of smell.

On the east coast, the Atlantic salmon moves into rivers in the spring to lay its eggs, too. But, unlike the salmon of the Pacific, Atlantic salmon do not die after their eggs are laid. They return to the sea and live to make other trips upstream to spawn.

Another ocean fish that moves in to fresh water to spawn is the river herring, or alewife. In Colonial days, the herring runs meant food and income for everyone, for they are good to eat fresh, and they keep well, pickled in brine or smoked and salted.

Many fishes make periodic migrations for spawning. Many move from the salt water of the sea into fresh water just as the salmon and the alewife do. The sturgeon, the shad, the

smelt, and the striped bass are some other ocean fishes that come in from the sea to spawn. Fishes that live in lakes and rivers may follow much the same migration pattern as the salmon and the alewife. The redhorse of freshwater lakes, as well as lake sturgeon, lake smelt, and the white sucker of the Mississippi, all move to tributary streams to spawn. Not many fishes move from fresh water to the ocean as the eel does.

Most fishes simply move from one part of a lake or river or ocean to another part for spawning. The haddock, the mackerel, the herring, and the cod all move in toward the coast to spawn.

Some of the richest fishing grounds in the world are over the shallow banks of the stormy North Atlantic, where these four fishes are abundant. There the water is rich in plankton, attracting herring and other plankton-eating fishes, as well as smaller animals that feed on plankton. The plankton feeders in turn become food for the haddock, the mackerel, and the cod. Even before there were any permanent settlements in the New World, European boats fished for cod in the banks off Newfoundland and Labrador. More than the alewife or any other fish, cod from the rich waters at their doorstep made New Englanders prosperous seafaring people.

Fishes also make periodic migrations for reasons other than to spawn. Many of their seasonal travels are for food or for water of the right temperature or saltiness. As a rule, fish move

Smelt, like many other ocean fishes, come in to fresh water to spawn.

Lamprey on lake trout

The lamprey has a suction-like mouth, teeth, and a rough tongue.

Adult lamprey

into deeper water in winter to escape the cold of the shallows near the coast. In spring they swim back toward shore. Food is more plentiful near shore. A great many fishes migrate on the heels of the migratory fishes that they prey on. Bluefish, for instance, follow herring. When fishermen find a school of herring, they can be quite sure of finding bluefish close behind.

The ocean is an immense fishpond. Fishermen must plan their schedule and set their course according to the migration habits of the fish they hope to catch. But it is not easy to learn the habits of fishes in the sea. Although fishermen have learned a great deal about fish travels, and in recent years thousands of fish have been tagged so

that their movements could be traced, there is still a great deal more to be learned about the migrations of fishes.

The travels of some fishes are important because of their effect on other fishes, especially those that are caught for food. The sea lamprey is such a fish. It migrates from the ocean into fresh-water streams and rivers to spawn, much as salmon do. As an adult, the lamprey is a parasite on other fishes. It fastens itself to another fish, rasps a hole with its tongue in its victim's body, and sucks the juices. The fish soon dies.

In some places, lampreys that hatched in tributary streams of the St. Lawrence River and Lake Ontario began to spend their adult years there instead of swimming out to sea. For a long time Niagara Falls kept the lamprey out of the other Great Lakes. But in 1829 the Welland Ship Canal was built around the falls, and eventually the lamprey found its way through the canal into the other lakes.

The lamprey lays its eggs in gravel nests in shallow, swift-flowing streams. In about a month the tiny larvae that hatch from the eggs drift downstream with the current. When they come to quiet water, the larvae sink to the bottom and burrow into the mud. After about five years, the young lampreys become dark blue on their backs and silvery beneath. They grow eyes and teeth and a file-like tongue. At flood time the lampreys swim downstream into the lake and move from one fish victim to another. After about two years they swim back upstream to spawn. They die soon afterward.

To save the lakes as fishing grounds, the United States and Canada began to study the habits of the lamprey to rid the lakes of them. Traps and dams were built and in some places electricity was used to stop lampreys moving upstream to spawn. Today, chemicals are used, too. These chemicals kill the lampreys without harming other fish. Some day the lakes may be cleared of lampreys and restocked with trout.

Lampreys spread from the St. Lawrence River into all of the Great Lakes.

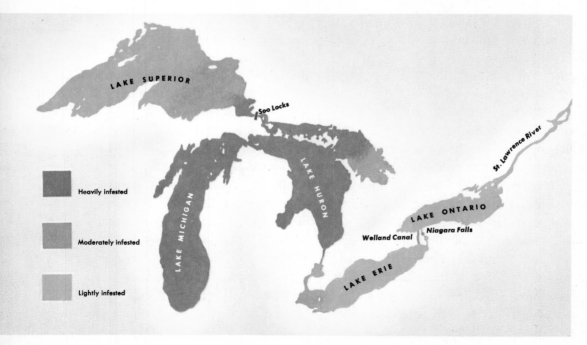

Amphibians and Reptiles

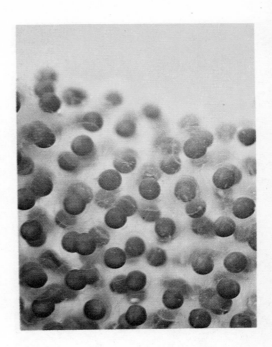

If a boy could jump in proportion to his size as far as some frogs and toads can, he could travel more than half a city block in just one jump. Throughout the ages toads and frogs have hopped their way around the world, although of course no one toad or frog ever made the whole trip by itself. Amphibians are not long-distance travelers. Many, however, do make short migrations at breeding time.

When spring comes, the toad that spends its summer in the garden snapping up flies hops off to find a pond or stream in which to lay its eggs. The tadpoles that hatch from the eggs have gills and must live in water. As they grow up, the tadpoles lose their gills and develop legs and lungs. Then they climb out of the water to live on land.

Frog tadpoles and young salamanders live in water just as toad tadpoles do. But most frogs and salamanders always stay so close to water that their trip is hardly more than one step and a plunge.

Reptiles are air-breathing animals all their lives. To lay their eggs they do not have to go in search of water as

Above, *frog eggs are protected by a gelatin coating.* Right, *newly hatched tadpoles have gills and must live in the water.*

A young frog develops lungs and legs and is able to live entirely out of water.

The tail of a growing frog shrinks gradually. When its tail is gone, the frog is an adult.

amphibians do. Not many reptiles are thought to travel more than a mile or two from their birthplace. But some reptiles—alligators and crocodiles, and some snakes and turtles—have taken to living in water. To lay their eggs these reptiles reverse the toad's migration pattern. At breeding time they leave the water and lay their eggs on shore.

The longest migration journeys made by any reptiles are those of the big turtles that live in the sea. Some sea turtles migrate hundreds of miles through the ocean between their feeding waters and the sandy shores where they lay their eggs. On some small islands near Borneo the coming of the green turtle to lay eggs is an astonishing sight. On moonlight nights dozens of these big turtles struggle up on shore to lay from 100 to 200 eggs apiece.

Both reptiles and amphibians are cold-blooded animals. No cold-blooded animals are active in cold weather. Most amphibians and reptiles hibernate. Usually, they do not go very far. Some bury themselves in mud at the bottom of ponds. Many work themselves deep into soft earth. Some snakes migrate in groups to dens, often returning to the same spot each year.

Birds

People once had rather odd explanations for the appearance and disappearance of certain birds in the spring and fall of the year. One idea was that some birds slept during the winter in hollow trees or in mud at the bottom of ponds. Another was that in winter birds changed into other kinds of birds. One of the more novel ideas was that birds left the earth in autumn and flew up to the moon to spend the winter.

When people gave up guessing about birds and began to keep careful records of what they saw, bird study became a science. Scientists now know a great deal about where birds go in winter, the paths they take, and when and how

Ducks are caught in a net at a bird refuge, then banded and released.

A lightweight aluminum band with a serial number is attached to a bird's leg. Most birds take banding calmly.

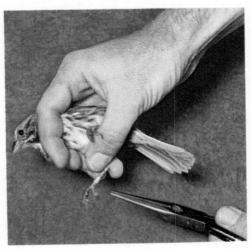

fast they travel. Much of what is known about the periodic migrations of birds has come from the practice of banding them. By fastening numbered bands about the legs of birds, scientists have learned a great deal, too, about such things as how long birds live, and where and how far young birds go when they leave the nest.

In North America there are now more than 2,000 stations where birds are caught in nets, banded, and then set free. Anyone who finds a bird, either living or dead, with a band on its leg, reports the number on the band to the U.S. Fish and Wildlife Service in Washington, D.C. and tells where and

31

The bristle-thighed curlew flies from Tahiti to the Arctic and nests in the forbidding tundra of inland Alaska.

ALASKA

5,500 miles

TAHITI

when the bird was found. By studying thousands and thousands of bird-banding reports, scientists can piece together the stories of the travels of each kind of bird.

Expeditions are another good way of learning about bird migrations. In 1948, American scientists traveled thousands of miles by boat, by plane, and finally on foot just to find the nesting place of the bristle-thighed curlew. This bird has been known to scientists since 1769, when Captain Cook found it on the island of Tahiti in the South

Pacific. A hundred years later the bird was again discovered, this time on the Alaskan coast. Scientists began to wonder if the bristle-thighed curlew, instead of nesting near Tahiti as they supposed it did, flew to far-off Alaska and raised its young there. It was not until the 1948 expedition that they could be certain of the curlew's long migration over the sea.

Of all the birds that migrate, none travels farther than the arctic tern. Each year this bird makes a round-trip journey of some 24,000 miles.

On their annual journeys south in the fall, both the arctic tern and the golden plover fly thousands of miles over the ocean.

Arctic terns nest in the Far North, in the long day of the arctic summer. In the fall they fly across the North Atlantic and then down the western coasts of Europe and Africa to regions in the far south. There, in the antarctic summer, they spend the winter.

The golden plover is another famous flyer. Part of its annual journey, too, is over the Atlantic. The plovers start their journey south from their arctic breeding grounds by flying southeast over Canada. From the Labrador coast they fly 2,400 miles over the ocean to the coast of South America. The rest of their way is over land. The birds stop in Argentina, some 8,000 miles from where they started. In March they fly back north. On the return trip the plovers do not follow the same path they take in autumn. In spring their trip is over land almost all the way. Then, instead of flying over the Atlantic, they fly northwestward over South America, across the Gulf of Mexico, up the Mississippi Valley, and northward over Canada. Young plovers follow this second path in both directions.

Many other birds, too, are long-distance travelers. But most birds that migrate make much shorter journeys. A great many of the birds that nest in northern states simply fly to regions along the Gulf in fall. Bluebirds from Massachusetts may spend the winter

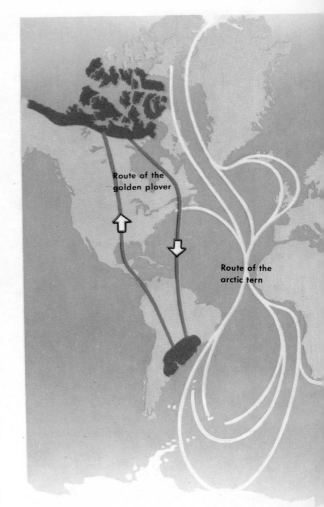

Route of the golden plover

Route of the arctic tern

in Georgia, and red-winged blackbirds from Minnesota may fly to Texas.

The summer and winter ranges of some birds may be so close together that they overlap. Where the ranges overlap the bird is found all year round. In Virginia, for instance, there are robins all year round, but they are not the same robins. Those that live there

33

The golden plover takes only 48 hours to cross the ocean.

The arctic tern flies tremendous distances.

in summer move farther south for winter, but their place is taken by other robins that move down from the north. No one robin has far to go. A bird with a large breeding range may simply crowd into the southern part of it for winter and spread out again in spring. The field sparrow has such a range.

Most people think that all birds that migrate fly south for the winter. Some birds, however, that nest high in mountains just move down the mountains to winter in nearby plains and foothills. In the Rockies, chickadees and juncos do just this. Such migration is called "vertical migration."

In the Southern Hemisphere there are birds that fly north for winter. The shining cuckoo spends summers in New Zealand and raises its young there. In March and April, when it is fall in New Zealand, these birds fly more than 2,000 miles north over the Pacific to pass the winter in the warmer climate of the Solomons.

Adélie penguins that nest in the Antarctic also move north in the fall. Penguins cannot fly but they are expert swimmers. Adélies spend the winter at sea. In spring they may have to walk 50 miles or more over frozen seas to reach their rookeries. Emperor penguins breed in Antarctica, too, but their journey is the reverse. They travel south in fall and hatch their chicks in the cold of the antarctic winter.

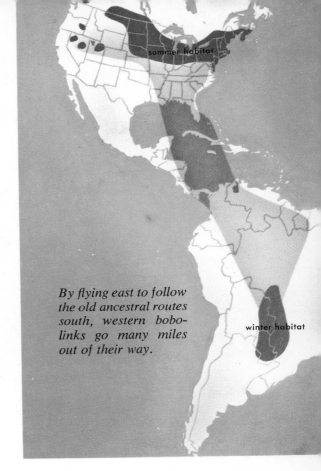

By flying east to follow the old ancestral routes south, western bobolinks go many miles out of their way.

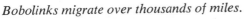

Bobolinks migrate over thousands of miles.

Some bird migrations in the tropics are movements between dry and wet seasons. One roller from Thailand flies more than a thousand miles to Borneo, then back again at breeding time. In the Western Hemisphere there are similar migrations within the tropics.

Through much of the year there is some movement of birds in and out of most regions. Some birds arrive late in spring and leave early in the fall. Some early birds, on the other hand, stay late in fall. In general, the birds that come late leave early, and those

35

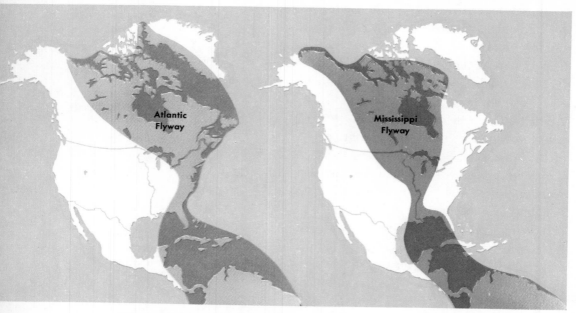

There are four main flying routes, or flyways, across North America.

that come early stay late. One reason is that often the early birds do not travel far. They can stay later because, like the bluebird that reaches St. Louis in February and stays almost through November, they do not have far to go for winter. When the bobolink reaches St. Louis in May, it has flown 5,000 miles to get there and has just as far to go when it leaves in September.

Anyone might expect that birds, in migrating long distances, would travel "as the crow flies." But bird-banding studies show that birds do not fly straight-line courses to their destinations. Inherited bird behavior leads each kind of bird to travel a set migration route established for it by genera-

tions of ancestors. Bird-banding studies show, too, that in North America all the many different migration routes of birds tend to feed into four great bands of skyway travel which are commonly called flyways.

As the map of the Atlantic Flyway above shows, routes leading from many different parts of North America lead into this great flyway. It includes the path out over the ocean that the golden plover follows south in fall. Few birds follow the plover's oversea route. Most birds of the Atlantic Flyway follow the coast. Some migrate only as far as the southern states. Others go on to Cuba and Jamaica. Some few go still farther, crossing 500 miles of

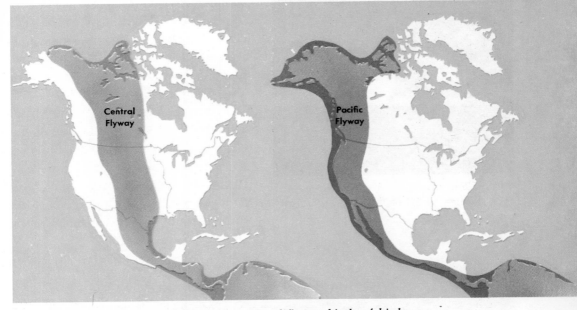

Each flyway is used by many different kinds of birds.

ocean between Jamaica and the South American coast. The bobolink is one that does. This step of the Atlantic Flyway is used by so few other birds that it is often called the "bobolink route." Most Atlantic Flyway birds that are headed for South America cross the handle of Florida and the Gulf of Mexico to Yucatan, and then travel on to South America over land.

The Mississippi Flyway is used by more birds than any of the other flyways. It includes the longest migration route of the Western Hemisphere, one that leads from Alaska's arctic coast to the tip of South America. Each spring and fall some shore birds fly its whole length. Barn swallows and nighthawks,

too, follow much of it. From the Arctic to the Gulf of Mexico, the Mississippi Flyway is a broad, easy skypath for birds. There is plenty of food and water. There are no mountains or deserts to cross. Much of the way there are trees that give shelter.

Most of the birds that travel the Mississippi Flyway stop and spend the winter in the Gulf states. Others stop even sooner. Robins and blue jays, for instance, flying south from Canada may stop in Illinois and spend the winter there. Of the multitudes of ducks and geese that use this flyway, a great many go to bird refuges in Arkansas and Louisiana. You might expect that land birds on their way to the tropics

37

The yellow warbler travels north so fast that it often arrives ahead of the spring.

would follow the Gulf coast and then fly south over land, but most of them do not. Instead, they strike off across the water. Even the tiny ruby-throated hummingbird crosses the Gulf in one long 500-mile flight.

Just to the west, between the Mississippi Valley and the Rockies, is the Central Flyway. Many water birds use it as well as land birds of the Great Plains. In the main, this is a direct pathway over land from the Far North straight south to Mexico and Central and South America.

Canada geese stop often to rest and feed during their migratory journey.

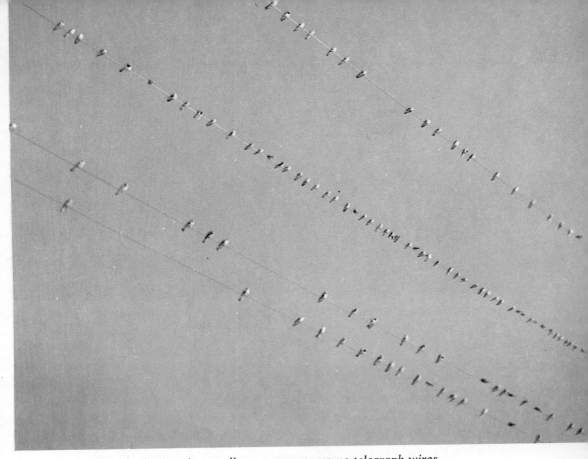

A flock of migrating swallows pauses on some telegraph wires.

The Pacific Flyway follows the west coast just as the Atlantic Flyway follows the east coast. In it are many routes that begin in western arctic regions and in the Rocky Mountains. Along the west coast the climate is mild even in winter. Many western birds do not migrate. Most of those that do, do not travel far, for there are suitable winter homes for birds from Puget Sound southward. Not many birds that use this flyway go far beyond Central America, where all four of the flyways merge into one.

The speed of migrating birds is no measure of how fast birds are able to fly. Most ducks and geese could do 500 miles a day rather easily. Migratory journeys, however, are much more leisurely than that. Usually, ducks and geese take several weeks to go a thousand miles. At some places they stop to rest and feed for several days before going on. Most small land birds, too, take their time in traveling.

People used to think that migrating birds flew at heights three miles or more above the ground. Now we know

39

A flock of redstarts darkens the skies as the birds continue their journey south.

that few birds ever fly higher than 3,000 feet and that most fly much lower. There is less oxygen higher up, and the air is too thin to support them.

Night travelers among bird migrants far outnumber those that travel by day. Almost all small land birds migrate at night. There is a good reason why. Flying uses up a great deal of energy. By traveling at night, birds are free to look for food in the daytime when they can see to find it. By flying at night, too, birds avoid many enemies. But some strong-flying land birds, such as swallows, swifts, and nighthawks that catch their insect food in the air as they travel, migrate in the daytime. So do many ducks and geese. Many water birds migrate both day and night.

For thousands of years people have wondered how birds find their way to distant places and how they know where to go when they first set out for places they have never been before. In repeating a journey, birds probably watch for landmarks, for they have good vision and good memories. Many follow coastlines and rivers that can be seen even on dark nights. But neither memory nor vision can be very helpful over the ocean or in a thick fog.

Many scientists think that birds that fly in the daytime navigate by the sun. In some experiments, starlings have been made to start off in the wrong direction by means of mirrors that changed the apparent direction of the light from the sun. In recent years scientists have experimented with caged birds under planetarium domes to see whether night flyers set their course according to the stars. Some of their findings seem to indicate that birds really may "read the stars."

Perhaps, some scientists say, the mysterious "sense of direction" of birds is located in the semicircular canals of the inner ear. The semicircular canals are the organs that give vertebrates their sense of balance. Some think that birds can sense the earth's magnetic fields through their semicircular canals. Others think that through the canals birds sense differences in what is called the Coriolis force, a force which results from the earth's spinning on its axis. Some think birds navigate by sensing both the magnetic and Coriolis forces in the semicircular canals.

In spite of all the experiments that have been done in the past 100 years to try to solve the puzzle of bird navigation, scientists have not yet come up with any explanation that is entirely satisfactory.

All along their way migrating birds run into danger. Thousands are killed every spring and fall. Storms take the heaviest toll. One fall, thousands of migrating juncos, wrens, thrushes, sparrows, warblers, and brown creepers were drowned when a sudden snowstorm over Lake Huron forced them down into the lake. Birds crossing the ocean may be blown into the water by strong storm winds. Often birds are driven far off course in windstorms.

Lighthouses, skyscrapers, tall bridge piers, and monuments are man-made obstructions that also may bring death to countless birds each spring and fall. Such obstacles equipped with fixed

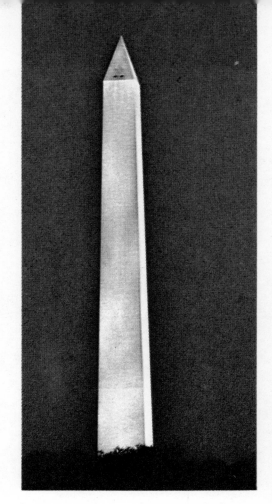

Brightly lit towers endanger night flyers.

white lights are more dangerous to birds than unlighted ones or those with red or flashing lights. A fixed white light seems to dazzle night-flying birds just as it does night-flying moths and beetles. Among 576 birds found dead at the foot of Washington Monument one September morning there were warblers, wrens, vireos, and tanagers.

Strangely enough, not many birds die of exhaustion from flying too long.

41

Range and migration route of the scarlet tanager. Most scientists believe that the development of the migration habit in birds is associated with the search for food.

gration of birds might have come about. According to one theory, the Northern Hemisphere was the ancestral home of birds that are now migratory. Long ago the climate there was warm, and there was enough food all year round. With the coming of the Ice Age, however, the birds were pushed south. For long periods of thousands of years at a time these birds lived in the south. But as the ice melted they could spread farther and farther north for a part of every year. Gradually, the habit of regular migrations became firmly fixed.

In another theory the tropics are thought to be the ancestral home of all birds. Over the ages the tropics became so filled with birds that there was not enough food for all of them. The overcrowding was especially bad at nesting time, for young birds eat a great deal. Gradually, the pressure of overcrowding pushed some birds farther and farther north each spring as the ice sheets melted back. In winter the birds that flew to nest in the north returned to the ancestral homeland in the tropics.

Both ideas could explain how some birds came to migrate. But neither one helps to explain the east-west migrations of birds in the tropics or the vertical migrations of mountain birds that move down for winter.

Birds are wonderful flying machines. Death from exhaustion is usually the result of unusual weather conditions or insufficient food.

Why does the scarlet tanager fly between regions thousands of miles apart each spring and fall? Why do so many other birds, too, fly between distant places every year while others do not? People have been almost as puzzled by why birds migrate as how birds are able to find their way.

Scientists have suggested several ideas to explain how the seasonal mi-

Mammals of the Sea

Through the winter months northern fur seals roam the ocean. But each spring they come together on the shores of the Pribilof Islands, some 200 miles west of Alaska in the Bering Sea. How the seals find these tiny island dots in the sea and arrive there right on schedule no one really knows.

The fur seals belong to a group called "fin-footed mammals." Instead of feet adapted to walking, the seals and their relatives have flippers, or "fins," for swimming. On land they are clumsy, dragging their heavy bodies along. And, although they live in the sea, they breathe air as other mammals do.

Every year, the fur seals arrive on the Pribilof Islands to spend the summer.

Much whaling goes on in polar seas where many kinds of whales migrate in summer to feed on plant and animal plankton.

The bulls arrive at the Pribilof Islands first, stake out homesites, and watch for the females. As the cows come ashore, each bull "landowner" herds as many cows as he can into his territory. An active bull may get for himself as many as 60 or 70 wives. The little black-coated seal pups are born several days to a few weeks after the cows arrive. The herd spend the summer on the rocky shores.

The bulls stand guard over their harems and fight off other, less successful bulls. The cows are busy with their pups. The pups must be fed and protected, and they must be taught how to swim. By late fall the breeding grounds are deserted and the seals have headed out to sea to roam about and feed on fish and squid until spring.

Some other fin-footed mammals, too, make long migrations through the ocean. The South American sea lion travels far and wide in the sea before it comes ashore to breed. Some harp seals, members of the true seal family, travel from Greenland waters to Spitsbergen and give birth to their snow-white pups on ice floes there. True seals, however, do not gather in large herds. Many of them never travel any distance from where they breed.

On some clear winter days, at a certain point overlooking San Diego Bay on the California coast, people can go and watch the whales swim by. Just a mile or two off the coast the gray whales pass on a long migration from their arctic feeding grounds to the place where they breed in quiet, protected bays off Lower California.

44

There the calves are born. The gray whales do not stay long in the shallow Mexican waters. By March or April they are on their way back to the Arctic to complete an annual round trip of some 12,000 miles.

A swim from the Arctic Circle to the Tropic of Cancer and back again may not be a surprising trip for a whale. Whales are wonderfully adapted for living and moving about in the sea. They are strong, swift swimmers that,

unlike seals, never come up on shore. Their young are born and nursed in the sea. But like seals, they must come up to the surface to get air, for they breathe with lungs.

Just why the gray whale goes where it does to bear its young is not clear. But it is not hard to understand why it returns to the Arctic to spend the summers. The gray whale feeds on plankton. And in summer the polar seas are rich in plankton. The part of the plankton which the gray whale eats is a small shrimp-like crustacean about half

an inch long called "krill." The krill are abundant because the tiny plankton plants they feed on grow and multiply so fast in the long hours of daylight in polar summers. Over great stretches of the ocean swarms of krill may be so thick that they give the water a reddish color. To eat, the gray whale has simply to browse near the surface through a swarm of krill and take in mouthfuls of water. Fringed plates of whalebone in its mouth strain out the krill when the whale expels the water from its mouth.

The blue whale, or sulphur bottom, is a giant relative of the gray whale. This big whale also migrates to polar seas in summer and feeds on krill. But people do not know very much about either the migration routes or the nurseries of the blue whale.

The horseshoe crab is another plankton animal when it is very young.

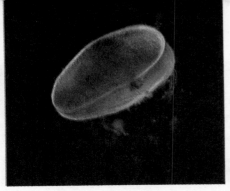

Young jellyfish, too, are common in plankton.

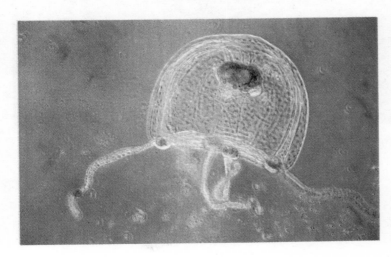

Ostracods are tiny crustaceans that are abundant in plankton.

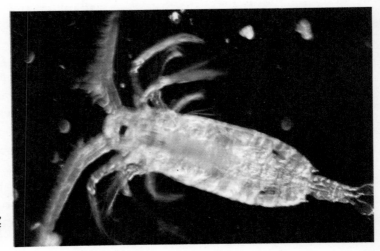

Another crustacean, the copepod, is part of the plankton mass.

47

Caribou travel south in vast herds, seeking sheltering forests for the winter.

Land Mammals

Many land mammals, too, move about in time with the seasons. But most land mammals must travel on foot. It is not surprising, then, that none make such long-distance journeys as the round trips of the bobolink and the gray whale.

The caribou of the barren grounds above the tree line in Canada and Alaska roam about in spring and summer feeding on the lichens, mosses, and grasses of the tundra and escaping as best they can the mosquitoes and flies that begin to swarm in the northern springtime. Many find relief in the

strong breezes blowing in from the sea along the arctic shores.

Caribou fawns are born in May. They are strong and hardy babies, not hurt by the cold and snow of the north. They can run fast behind their mothers when they are only a few hours old.

By mid-summer the caribou begin to gather in vast winding herds and travel south from the tundra to the evergreen forests where they spend the winter. When a herd is overtaken by early winter storms, the animals look for some protected place and crowd tightly together. The moisture in their

48

breath forms a cloud about the herd which holds in the heat from their bodies as in a closed room.

Many other plant eaters move from summer pasture when winter comes. The wapiti, or elk, of Yellowstone National Park move down from the higher valleys to spend the winter in the valley of Jackson Hole. In former years, when great herds of American bison roamed the western plains, the fall migration southward of vast herds of bison was one of the most spectacular sights of the West.

In warm regions many mammals, like birds, migrate each year to escape the dry season, just as in the north some move to escape the cold of winter. In Africa antelopes and zebras gather in herds and leave the hot, dry grasslands. Elephants move up into high mountain forests or into thick forests that grow along the rivers.

Bats are the only mammals with wings. They can fly long distances easily and quickly just as birds can. Many northern bats fly to warm regions for winter. Bats in Canada may travel as far south as the Bermudas. And, like many invertebrates, amphibians, and reptiles, bats that live in regions of cold winters may hibernate through the long period when food is scarce. Some bats travel long distances to caves where they hibernate together in tremendous numbers.

African elephants move into the forests to escape the dry seasons on the plains.

Man

Early man depended on the seasons for his comfort and his food just as wild animals do today. For thousands of years man must have moved about, following the animals he hunted in time with the seasonal rhythm of the years. Long after people learned to keep their own flocks and herds for meat and milk, some men still moved with the seasons, pitching their tents wherever there was grass for their animals. In some places even now there are nomad peoples.

Such human travels are quite different from the seasonal journeys of birds and whales and fishes. People do not inherit a migratory habit; nor have they, so far as we know, an inborn sense of direction that tells them where

to go and how to find the way without map or compass.

The migrations that have meant most for mankind have been movements that eventually spread people far and wide over the earth. The earliest migration that scientists know much about was one that brought people into the New World for the first time. It started late in the Ice Age, many thousands of years before Columbus, when Old Stone Age hunters wandered out of Asia into Alaska across what is now Bering Strait. Scientists do not know who these ancient people were, exactly where they came from, or why they came. But from the record of old camping grounds, scientists can trace part of their movements as they slowly

Even today there are still some peoples who, like these Kurds, constantly move with the seasons in search of grass and water for their flocks.

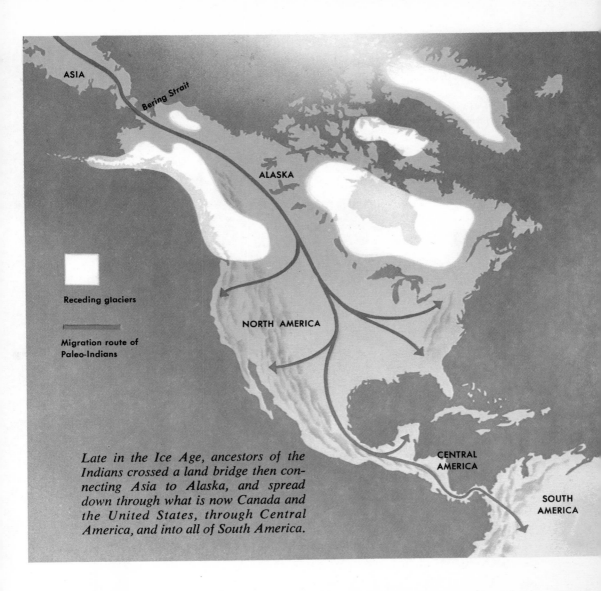

ASIA

Bering Strait

ALASKA

Receding glaciers

Migration route of
Paleo-Indians

NORTH AMERICA

CENTRAL
AMERICA

SOUTH
AMERICA

*Late in the Ice Age, ancestors of the
Indians crossed a land bridge then connecting Asia to Alaska, and spread
down through what is now Canada and
the United States, through Central
America, and into all of South America.*

spread southward, generation by generation, through corridors between the
last melting ice sheets of the Ice Age.
These first Americans were the ancestors of the Indians.

Old Stone Age men also spread
into Australia late in the Ice Age, but

they did not reach the tiny islands out
in the Pacific. Nor did Old Stone Age
people spread into the Arctic. The
people who settled in the Arctic and
became the Eskimos went there only
3,000 years or so ago. And the people
we call Polynesians found and settled

51

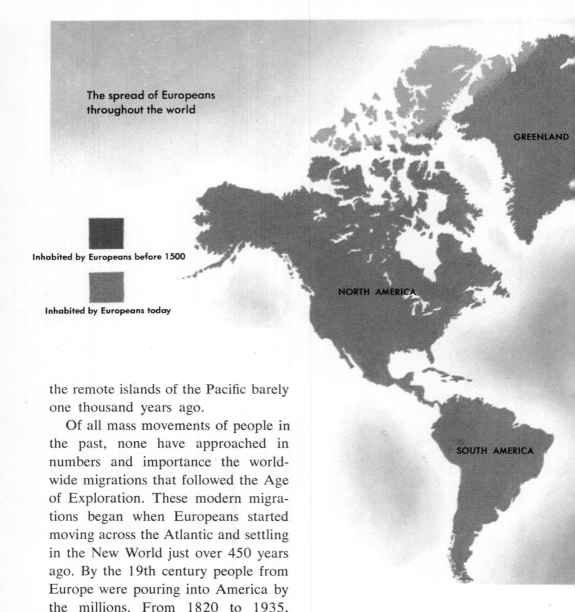

The spread of Europeans throughout the world

GREENLAND

Inhabited by Europeans before 1500

Inhabited by Europeans today

NORTH AMERICA

SOUTH AMERICA

the remote islands of the Pacific barely one thousand years ago.

Of all mass movements of people in the past, none have approached in numbers and importance the world-wide migrations that followed the Age of Exploration. These modern migrations began when Europeans started moving across the Atlantic and settling in the New World just over 450 years ago. By the 19th century people from Europe were pouring into America by the millions. From 1820 to 1935, more than 35 million Europeans settled in the United States alone. In the same period some 4 million settled in Australia and more than a million migrated to South Africa. Within the past 40 years millions from Russia migrated into northern Asia.

Other races, too, have moved about in recent centuries. The migration of Europeans to the Americas brought

52

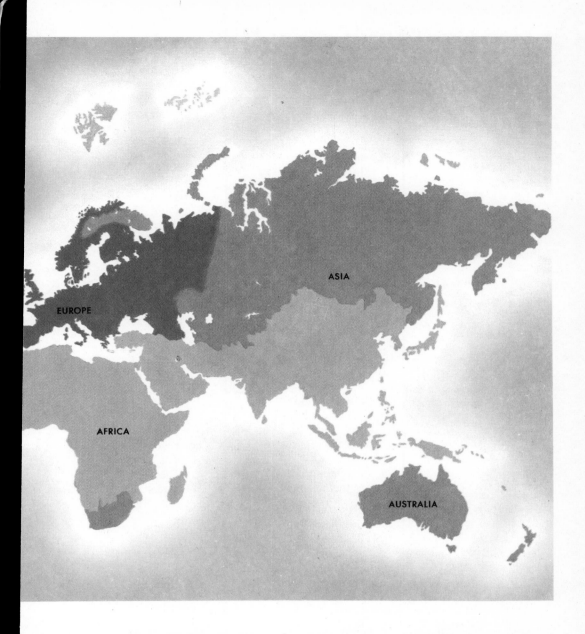

ASIA

AFRICA

AUSTRALIA

with it a movement of more than 15 million Negroes out of Africa. The Chinese spread into southeast Asia, the East Indies, the Philippines, and the Hawaiian Islands. After 1857, when Japan first began to play a part in world affairs, the Japanese, too, spread into other lands. Today, all the major races of man make their home on every continent except Antarctica.

53

Index

PICTURE CREDITS. *The National Audubon Society:* W. T. Davidson, cover (bot.), pp. 10 (a), 23 (top); Philip M. Smith, p. 7; Stephen Collins, pp. 10 (f), 31; Lynwood Chace, p. 10 (b); Dr. William J. Jahoda, p. 10 (e); Dick Hanley, p. 11; Hal. H. Harrison, pp. 10 (d), 15, 38; George P. Lower, p. 18; Roy Pinney, p. 21; Karl W. Kenyon, p. 43. *American Museum of Natural History:* Herbert Birrell, cover (center), p. 49; F. H. Pough, p. 12; James E. Thompson, p. 16 ; Steve McCutcheon, pp. 23 (bot.), 24, 26, 48; Dr. Arthur A. Allen, pp. 32, 35, 40; Stanwood C. Feiker, cover (top), pp. 9, 34 (top); Dr. Roman Vishniac, pp. 46, 47; Werner Bischof, *Magnum,* p. 24; Russ Kinne, pp. 24, 38; Rutherford Platt, p. 6; *Camera Clix,* p. 17; S. C. Wilson, p. 19; John W. Green, p. 20; Northern Color Film Co., Cooper Landing, Alaska, pp. 23 (center), 34 (bot.); Oregon State Highway Dept., p. 25; William A. Amox, pp. 29, 30; Canadian Wildlife Service, p. 31; Fred J. Moroon, p. 41; *Monkmeyer,* Don Woolridge, p. 39, Boubab, p. 50; D. Richard Statile, p. 45. Drawings on pp. 22, 27 by James Gordon Irving from *Fishes, A Golden Nature Guide.*

A